Avoiding Mistakes & CRUSHING Your Deals
Using Your VA Loan

Winning Strategies for Veterans Buying, Selling & Refinancing Homes

Tad,

Thanks for all you do!

Peter Van Brady

Best Wishes,

Peter

This book may be purchased for educational, business or promotional use. For information, please contact or write:

Media

SoCalVAHomes

30448 Rancho Viejo Road, Suite 120

San Juan Capistrano, CA 92675

888-556-2018

This publication is intended to provide accurate and authoritative information in regard to the subject matter covered. It is sold with the understanding that the author, publisher and affiliates are not engaged in rendering professional, legal, accounting, or investing services. When expert assistance is required in these disciplines, the services of a competent professional should be sought.

ISBN-13: 978-1541248700

ISBN-10: 1541248708

Praise for: *Avoiding Mistakes & CRUSHING Your Deals Using Your VA Loan*

"Avoiding Mistakes & Crushing Your Deals Using Your VA Loan is a valuable read for Veterans trying to achieve their own unique real estate goals. I speak from personal experience with the author when I say Peter Van Brady has crafted a field manual for success in real estate, lending and personal finance for our community." - E. A. "Dusty" Rhodes, (former) Force Protection Manager, Naval Anti-Terrorism, U. S. Navy

"Avoiding Mistakes & Crushing Your Deals Using Your VA Loan is extremely thorough. It's very good information that answers every question any Veteran or military person would want to know about using their VA benefits to successfully achieve their financial goals in real estate." – Colonel Richard Williams, U.S.A.F., Real Estate Investor

"Avoiding Mistakes & Crushing Your Deals Using Your VA Loan breaks down a wealth of knowledge into manageable sections and provides Veterans with not only the essential knowledge to complete transactions successfully but also gives great information on the nuances of gaining the competitive advantage in today's market! My wife and I would know after three rewarding transactions with the author." – Sgt. William Bauer U.S.M.C.

"Avoiding Mistakes & Crushing Your Deals Using Your VA Loan is the ultimate 'VA field guide' for how to succeed in purchasing

and refinancing homes for active military and Veterans. Everyone can learn a valuable nugget from this Encyclopedia!" – Sgt. Steve Schiefer, U.S.A.F.

"*Avoiding Mistakes & Crushing Your Deals Using Your VA Loan* is an excellent one-stop-shopping tool for all things home-buying for Veterans! This book is written in such a way that even someone who has never been through the process of purchasing a home can clearly understand it. An invaluable resource for service members navigating the waters of home-buying." - Master Chief Alicia Harrison, U. S. Navy

"*Avoiding Mistakes & Crushing Your Deals Using Your VA Loan* is a book that we can truly appreciate. Let's face it. Military does not stay in one place long. Several topics covered in this book have been discussed by us many times because of our personal experience of having been an owner more than once and a renter as well. This book will help answer a lot of questions people have about financing with a VA loan." – Sallie Johnson & Colonel Terry Johnson, U.S.M.C.

CONTENTS

Core Values & Distinguished Mission: To do what no other company can do…to do what no other company is willing to do for our men and women who serve…to be the ultimate crusaders for Veterans buying homes.

Section I   Basic Training for Winning on a VA Home Purchase

Should you continue to rent…or should you be buying a home using your VA Home Loan Benefit?

The nuts, bolts, and key ingredients of a successful home purchase using your VA Home Loan Benefit.

How to get your Certificate of Eligibility and why ALL this documentation is so important to using your VA Home Loan Benefit.

Section II Special Ops: Advanced Tools for a VA Home Purchase

Section III The Surprising Truth About Your Credit Scores

Section IV More Winning (and Losing) Strategies for Using Your VA Benefits

Are bi-weekly payments on your mortgage a trick?

Why receiving disability income is an economic advantage for VA home loan borrowers, especially when getting a cash-out VA refinance loan.

The pros and cons of financing options when making home improvements or consolidating your debt.

An in depth examination of the benefits and pitfalls of this new home improvement financing gadget

When should you refinance your VA home loan? The tremendous advantages of a VA IRRRL – Interest Rate Reduction Refinance Loan

Your VA Home Loan Benefit offers $6000 for energy efficient home improvements. Why?

Section V Winning The BIG Game With Your VA Benefits

Acknowledgements

This book was an effort that took more than three years. I hope to get the next one done in less than two! It is as much an "FAQ book" for Veterans as it is a manuscript for explaining my beliefs on how to structure personal finances to build security and wealth, and it includes easy tools and techniques to utilize toward that goal. Over time, anyone can do it.

My wife of 25 years, Nancy has endured my endless long work hours into the night and through the weekends, as I have built my small businesses over the decades. Equally, if not more important, is her incredibly valuable contribution as my primary editor of this book. She forced me to invest a significant amount of energy to crystallize the presentation of many of the technical concepts into their current form. Without her filter, many of the chapters which discuss investing, real estate investing and mortgage banking would be less valuable to you. And my kids, Chelsea, Nicholas and especially Mia, demonstrated an ample amount of patience with me as I worked through endless weekends.

My mother in law, Mary Jean Tibbels, with a career as an English teacher, was gracious enough to perform one of the final edits. Thanks MJ. You are the best, and you know it!

My associate Barry Harrington was helpful in organizing some of the initial content. That exercise proved to be "process intensive," presenting its own set of challenges. Thank you for your contributions my old friend.

My associate Brandon Breshears always had supportive comments and encouraged the completion of this project in the context of the goals of SoCalVAHomes. Thanks Mr. B!

My partner Shawn Swaroop has always been "The Rock." He and I co-founded our mortgage company, One Touch Lending, in 1996. He has been the most stable influence on my career and the kindest human you will ever meet. He is an asset in anyone's life and a mentor without trying.

Overview – How to Use This Book!

This book is organized into sections which progress from the basics of using your VA home loan benefit to buy a home, to advanced concepts in financial planning and real estate investing, to starting your own business.

It's an "FAQ book" for active military families and Veterans that offers something for everyone for every circumstance. I wouldn't expect you to read it cover to cover.

I hope that you will browse the Table of Contents and find a topic that interests you and obtain answers your specific questions. I expect you to, ultimately, master the financial concepts contained within. Your long-term financial heath depends on it.

You'll notice some of the chapters are brief and some are extremely deep and broad in their scope. The brief chapters cover important topics that are the "fundamentals" to attaining long-term financial success. The long chapters tend to reflect a deeper passion that I have for the subject matter. Study the long chapters. Implement the concepts within. You won't be disappointed in the results!

Our Story: The Big Idea Becomes A Reality

SoCalVAHomes' Core Values & Distinguished Mission: To do what no other company can do...to do what no other company is willing to do for our men and woman who serve...to be The Ultimate Crusaders for Veterans buying homes.

In 1991, I married my college sweetheart and was working in the loan industry. Along my career path, I was fortunate to meet a variety of people who provided opportunities to learn and grow in the financial services industry. In 1996, I opened my mortgage company One Touch Lending with my partner Shawn Swaroop. Together, we grew our families and grew our business. One Touch Lending began working with Veterans after 9-11. That horrific event altered my career path, pointing me in a direction which I wouldn't fully understand until several years later. In the fall of 2008, I started a real estate investment company called SARTRE, LLC. We purchased thousands of distressed properties and apartment units with cash in hopes of selling them at higher prices. Then in 2011, I had an "aha moment" to combine the resources of One Touch Lending and SARTRE to create SoCalVAHomes.org and our Dreamweaver Home Purchase Process ^{TM} which delivers a fully custom renovated home to active military and Veterans for no money down and no closing costs.

I originally chronicled our story, from inception to evolution, titled *Rewriting the Rules: The SoCalVAHomes.org Story*. That document is now available on our website where it highlights my story and SoCalVAHomes' unique vision for our clients, the VA home buyer. This book that you are currently reading is the extension of my story, and this book's intent is to provide answers to frequently asked questions by Veterans who want to become homeowners, become investors and who want to create wealth.

The history of SoCalVAHomes is of course interconnected with my own biography. My son Nick has autism, and my wife Nancy has been running his home educational program since he was a toddler. Nancy was fortunate to hire an aide for Nick named Michelle. And at the time, Michelle was dating a young man who she claimed was a genius at real estate (and other things), and she kept *insisting* that I meet him and interview him. I said, "Nah, I don't need to hire anyone right now." But one thing led to another and three months later, I hired her boyfriend, Brandon Breshears. as my loan production assistant, and boy, was Michelle right! Brandon moved beyond his initial responsibilities quickly. "Young Skywalker," as I used to refer to him, is a genius in so many ways, and he infected me with an extra dose of enthusiasm that only someone who is twenty years my junior could be capable of! Brandon and I shared the same dedication and motivation in helping Veterans achieve homeownership, which in turn, propelled forward the goals of SoCalVAHomes. I was very fortunate to work with Brandon. He was a valuable contributor for a myriad of reasons, including tech expertise, experience in construction, and property valuation.

I had that lightning bolt moment in the spring of 2011, and I was struck with "The Big Idea" of a unique business model that eventually became the Dreamweaver Home Purchase Process™ of SoCalVAHomes. At the time, I was monitoring the effects of recent interest rate declines on the housing market. The drop in rates created more affordable mortgage payments, resulting in an increase in home purchases, and VA buyers began to buy houses again in large numbers. As rates kept dropping, I refinanced hundreds of VA clients' loans from 6% down to 4%. I literally spoke to hundreds of clients about what they did and didn't get out of their home purchase, and I reviewed their finances in detail.

"The Big Idea" business model was to create a fully custom renovated home, a Veteran's dream home, which we would purchase with cash, renovate to their specifications and liking, and then sell to the Veteran using 100% VA financing with no out of pocket costs.

That effectively enabled the Veteran to have all the buying power of a cash buyer.

When buying homes, Veterans are often at a disadvantage in the real estate marketplace. Real estate agents and sellers prefer cash buyers and conventional buyers who can offer faster closings and substantial good faith deposits securing the commitment to close. The marketplace is typically unreceptive of requests for closing costs from VA buyers. The market is also aware of VA appraisal restrictions, longer time frames to obtain financing, and generally a lower probability of success when entertaining an offer to purchase from a VA home buyer.

SARTRE, LLC was looking for a way to enhance our real estate investment business in California. So, I surveyed my clients and asked them, "What if you could buy a fully custom renovated home instead of being turned away because your VA Loan puts you at a disadvantage in a marketplace that prefers cash and fat conventional offers?" 100% of my clients and prospects answered with a resounding "YES, YES! Where were you when I bought my home?" "The Big Idea" then became our business plan. SoCalVAHomes makes cash offers to purchase the home on behalf of Veterans, then renovates it the way they want it with upgrades and features they choose, and then sells it directly to the Veteran who uses their VA Home Loan Benefit to close, with zero down and zero closing costs.

In the spring of 2011, there were more foreclosures available at what appeared to be discount prices. Two years later in 2013, the market had turned into a seller's market, and inventory of homes for sale decreased dramatically. As a result, fewer homes that presented "renovation opportunities" were available for sale. So in an effort to always re-write the rules and provide our Veterans with the best options available in a competitive real estate market, we launched our Veteran's Angel Program ^{SM}. With this program, SoCalVAHomes represents our client as a traditional real estate agent would, making a "VA offer" but with some innovative, high-performance additives! The Veteran's Angel Program ^{SM} deploys three, very stealth and powerful tactics to secure purchase contracts while making a "VA offer" on behalf of our VA buyers.

What I've learned through the whole process of refinancing hundreds and hundreds of VA homeowners, and now working with a volume of VA purchase transactions, is that **the VA market is tremendously underserved**! There might be a handful of lenders who claim to only serve Veterans, but there is no real estate company that I'm aware of, anywhere in the country, that exclusively sells homes to Veterans. And there is a very good reason for this disinterest in the real estate community. It would be a tremendously risky and herculean task to build such a real estate company on a national level. To have success, you'd have to work in a marketplace, such as Southern California or South Florida where the concentration of VA buyers is high, relative to the total volume of transactions. For instance, in Southern California, in the Temecula Valley, the amount of VA transactions is literally 20% of the marketplace thanks to the Marines at Camp Pendleton and to the Navy in San Diego AND all the Veterans from both. That's a really high concentration of VA buyers.

However, imagine you're a real estate agent working only with active military and Veterans. You are often facing the most difficult and stringent transactions due to the VA appraisal process and VA underwriting criteria. VA loans are often the riskiest loans to get into escrow and to close, and the clientele you are servicing often has the least amount of money for down payments and reserves. And with government loans such as FHA and VA, clients often have lower credit scores than conventional borrowers. Collectively, all these factors combined are the reasons that listing agents and sellers prefer to stay away from VA homebuyers in general. This creates a steep, up-hill battle for the agent or real estate company that may wish to be "exclusive" and only represent this community of buyers.

To serve those who are currently underserved, our VA home buyers, a company would need to have exclusive realtors all over the country or region that only do VA business. Such a company doesn't exist and most likely, won't open due to these stumbling blocks. If you are going to build a business with active military and Veterans, you're really choosing to work with the most challenging group of clientele out there! Business builders typically choose an easier path, not the path of greatest resistance! And it's just not practical on a national level. A few individual agents in random markets might choose to cater to VA buyers as a percentage of their total transaction volume, but no one is going to devote a season of their career, let alone their entire career, to just serving VA buyers. That could be described as business suicide. Ironically, this is exactly what SoCalVAHomes has chosen to do!

Embarking upon such a challenge would have been impossible if I didn't first have a jump-start with several hundred VA refinance customers in my client list. In addition, my experience in VA financing with my mortgage company and a successful real estate investment company that has cash to spend buying homes was necessary to facilitate the business model and make the process successful. Finally, my team of knowledgeable experts who know how to evaluate homes, buy homes, and renovate homes on budget was already in place and ready to serve VA clients. With these strengths, SoCalVAHomes is able to successfully serve our VA buyers in this unique way. We are choosing to do what most people would consider business insanity.

So why are we on this mission to serve our active military and Veterans in a way they are not being served now? It's a question I ask myself all the time because the answer digs deep down into the source of my motivation. First, it frankly just seemed like a great idea! My associate Brandon and I had a blast just dreaming of such a company. "What if we could pull this off? What a great end result, and for the most deserved of people." *Serving men and women, who literally sacrificed careers, sacrificed everything to serve our country, serving this community,* certainly stirred a wave of patriotic feelings in our souls.

These feelings grew deeper until we were on a mission. We executed several "fully custom renovated home" transactions which were very, very difficult. It was both taxing and exhilarating at the same time. Purchasing a home, renovating it, managing the expectations of our clients, and creating financing that they were pleased with was a monumental task. Unfortunately, there are so many moving parts in such a transaction that several things could go wrong. Yet, part of our Client Induction Process is to describe all those moving parts, so that SoCalVAHomes and the homebuyers really become like partners. All parties move with the objective of creating a fully custom renovated home for the VA buyer. The work can be a nightmare of making custom renovation choices, adhering to timeframes, working with contractors, and staying on budget. But I love a huge challenge. I've always been a hard worker in everything I've done in my career, especially in real estate and the mortgage business, and I love doing things that others think can't be done. Sometimes, taking an idea from concept to execution is just a matter of working hard and getting it done.

I'll never forget presenting our first, fully custom renovated home to Brian and Lisa Doudera, from Imperial Beach, California. They got an incredible deal! They were paying $2200 in rent for an 1800 square foot property. SoCalVAHomes helped them own their new home with an $1800 mortgage payment and 2300 square feet of living space. They also got $8000 worth of appliances AND $20K worth of equity, all for zero down and zero closing costs! But the best was fulfilling Brian's request for a flat screen TV. "Could we include that in the renovations," he asked? The look on Brian's face when he saw that $5000, 80 inch, SHARP LCD TV on the wall was priceless! He asked for it...we delivered!

They were in awe...speechless...in disbelief and more than THRILLED!

For me, it was the best day of my career.

And I was looking to repeat that experience.

We were onto something big.

I didn't serve. My father served in the Army in the 1950's in the Korean War as an accountant. My father-in-law served in the Vietnam War as a flight surgeon in the Air Force and saw some combat. My interest in the experience of the American soldier and being in the U.S. armed services grew and grew, in part due to getting to know so many admirable people who did serve – our clients. I began to read books:

War by Sebastian Junger; also made into the documentary movie *Restrepo, Korengal* and more.

American Sniper, by Chris Kyle.

Lone Survivor, by Marcus Luttrell

13 Hours, by Mitchell Zuckoff (an account of the Benghazi attack)

For Love of Country, by Howard Schultz (founder of Starbucks)

Always Forward, Always Faithful, by Dick Couch (former Navy Seal and prolific author)

Fearless, by Eric Blehm – SEAL Team SIX's Adam Brown's life story, an inspiration to all Americans

I gained much admiration and appreciation for all branches of the military, especially the Special Forces. The amazing and selfless acts of valor by all service people still leave me in awe. The brutal conditions under which they so incredibly and valiantly protect our country are shocking. Their commitment appears unparalleled by anything in civilian society. The few books I've read are packed full of just horrendous accounts, in the context of incredible human interest stories about the attitude for service that soldiers and other people have, about their experiences, and about how they live their life in that manner.

I almost became jealous of the camaraderie that is shared and the adrenaline that is experienced. If you ask a combat solider about the most incredible emotional experience they have ever had and are willing to share, they will probably tell you that it was in the midst of a serious firefight - mortal combat - making decisions regarding the possible sacrifice of their life for the life of their buddies. I don't think you could imagine a situation anywhere on the planet were you could admire someone more. What a "steel-wrapped" bond, born of intense adrenaline and camaraderie.

When I start adding all of this up, it makes me feel really small. It makes me feel *insignificant* in comparison to the people out there who really commit to lives and careers of service. They choose to serve perhaps because they love it, and because they get so much out of it. So, what drives me and my company forward is literally the ability and the challenge to go "there" and do things in the marketplace that no one else will do, no one else will choose to do, and no one else *can* do because they are not in the position to do it. Because most of all, this effort is about serving our community - a difficult one to serve. The economics and logistics are very challenging. I feel compelled to rise to this challenge and to do what has never been done before, in service of those who have served. And you might have noticed the word Veteran has been capitalized. *As it relates to book, the word and title, Veteran, will always be capitalized no matter where it appears in a sentence. I believe that it is a title of honor and respect.*

We're on a mission to fill a need. We are very fortunate to have the resources to do it, and it's a whole hell of a lot of fun. Come join us on the ride!

Chapter 1: The Rational Renter vs. The Bold Buyer

Should you continue to rent or should you be buying a home using your VA Home Loan Benefit?

Once you are aware that you can buy a home without a down payment using your VA Home Loan Benefit, you will have to consider whether or not you are emotionally and financially ready for homeownership. The truth is there are advantages and disadvantages in both cases for buying or renting a house, and there are solid arguments for each.

So, just for compare and contrast purposes, let's look at both the upside and even the downside of homeownership. What are the pros? What are the cons? You may ask yourself:

- Am I ready for this major investment?
- Is purchasing a home the best use of money in my/our situation at this particular time?
- Do I need a house, or is a rental a wise choice *in my/our situation at this particular time*?
- Do I like the town or city and state where I am considering this purchase well enough to live there for years or decades?
- Am I financially biting off more than I can chew?
- Will my income grow, decrease, or be eliminated? What is my job security?
- What are my options?

- What are my goals, plans, financial health, interests?
- Do I want the responsibility of maintaining a piece of property?
- Do I envision myself spending my free time doing upkeep, or would I rather not have my weekends booked with chores?
- Is the house big enough?
- Is the house too big?
- Will it be enough if we start a family?
- Do we want children? Is this the right place to raise them?
- How are the local schools?

Advantages of the Homeownership Experience

The homeownership experience includes a host of awesome benefits including but not limited to:

- Pride of ownership, security, and increased privacy.
- Ability to landscape or decorate as you wish.
- A stable environment for your marriage and children. Owning a home is still a good investment, despite the housing bubble burst. Studies have shown that owning a house has numerous benefits, including a sense of well-being. Ownership also is a foundation for wealth creation, a vehicle to create equity, often your largest investment and asset in a portfolio. A house creates stability for you and your family, and stability in turn is known to be a factor in children doing better in school and having quality friendships as part of a community.
- You can own a dog (or other treasured pet). Try securing a rental as a pet owner--that's a real challenge!
- Houses usually increase in their value over time, making them not only a good residence, but good investments.

- Your mortgage payment, especially if on a 30 year fixed-rate, is a stable amount, unlike your rent costs which can vary year-to-year due to inflation, the supply and demand of rental property, or the whims of a landlord.

Tax incentives include:

- Tax breaks on the profit (when selling and repurchasing).
- Mortgage interest tax deduction.
- County real estate tax deduction.
- Credit on energy efficient home improvements.
- Savings/investments in the form of equity buildup.
- Huge tax credits on solar energy.

Disadvantages of Homeownership

Disadvantages are relative—Do you remember the saying "One person's trash is another person's treasure?" What you may consider a disadvantage may be what someone else considers an advantage. You might have dreams of travel or of someday living in a different state, so "long term commitment" to a property might be a problem for you. Another person may wish with all their heart to put down roots in a community for a lifetime or generations. One person's disadvantage is another person's advantage. Other disadvantages include:

- Long term commitment to property and town/city/state (ability to move or travel becomes limited).
- No longer can call the landlord when things go wrong.

- House and property maintenance is now up to you. Do you have the money and skills needed for repair and upkeep?
- Given many historical reference points in many areas across the country, there's an argument that says it can often be more expensive to own initially, but that's definitely not always the case. In certain areas at certain times, either renting or buying can be a better deal. While there are numerous Rent v. Buy calculators out there across the web, you could simply seek insight by calling us, SoCalVAHomes.
- There's the possibility of foreclosure, if you fail to keep current with your monthly mortgage. Simply, the bank (or lender) can take away your home. We hope you never face this situation. The loss of your home, of your investment, could then also result in other losses including your credit rating…not to mention the stress and strain on your life and relationships.

Advantages to Renting a House

- There are less responsibilities when you rent.
- If your toilet overflows or your heater breaks down in the dead of winter, you don't have to fix it yourself or pay for home maintenance costs out of your own pocket.
- If utilities are covered in your rent, you save additional money.
- Landlord takes care of repairs and maintenance.
- You are more flexible with a short-term commitment when you rent, enabling you to move if you need or want to.

Disadvantages to Renting a House

- There are no tax breaks when you rent.

- There is no way to build equity when you rent.
- Housing costs are not fixed, and most rents rise annually, with inflation.
- Because of the nature of renting (large turnover, the owner's need to get into the property for repairs and upgrades, the potential that the house's owner may sell or die,) you might be told you have to move even when you don't want to.

It might seem that renting and homeownership are not that different, when you consider a case by case basis such as the one above. However, the majority of the time homeownership is the smartest decision you can make, especially if you have the advantage of the VA Home Loan Benefit. Your own educated, common sense will ultimately be the most important influence on your decision to "own or rent." What is your goal, your dream? Do you want the freedom that rentals allow you? Or do you want the benefits that only homeownership can bring? There may be a time when renting works better for you, but it is most likely a time where you are struggling, indecisive, between life milestones, or not living in the region you most prefer. Again, owning a home is the best investment you can make, if you can afford it. Learn how to afford it.

Americans like homeownership. Prior to the financial crisis in 2008, a record high 69.2% of Americans owned homes. When the housing bubble burst and the most severe crisis since the Great Depression upended the economy, seven million Americans lost their homes. In 2014 in America, homeownership is at 65.4%, a large figure indeed. If two-thirds of the country own homes, even in hard times, it suggests that it is a strong national value.

Statistics are often hard to interpret. For example, reading that 75% of Americans are well-fed doesn't help when you realize that

25% are hungry. But in America, again, 65.4% of our population own homes. That's a big number. America is such a diverse nation now that it is amazing that <u>anything</u> ranks that high. To put that statistic in perspective—just for fun—let's compare 65.4% to other percentages of basic American behaviors, possessions, and/or values.

Percentage of Americans who are:

Left-handed	10%
Overweight	35.5%
Married	51%
Democrat	31%
Republican	29%
Independent	38%
Blue-eyed	33.8%
Illiterate	14%
Prefer Pepsi over Coke	23%
Unable to swim	36%

So...65.4% is a big number! 65.4% of Americans who value homeownership enough to be a homeowner against all odds says something powerful – a real testimony about its importance and worth – the institution of homeownership!

Yet nothing is simple, especially in the aftermath of the financial crisis. You most likely believe, bone-deep, that renting is cheaper than buying, and that it is a natural procession to move from renting to buying. Most of us have forever internalized the American Dream of owning a house and a piece of land. The equation for that dream didn't used to be so complex. But things have changed.

If you were one of the seven million Americans who lost your home, what would you do? Besides perhaps being embroiled in perpetual frustration, you would most likely go find a place to RENT.

The equation of rent vs. buy has changed because so many of your fellow Americans who were tossed out of their homes in the Great Recession, are now renting! Just try to find a rental in 2014! The law of supply and demand is assuredly at work, and the homes usually available to people who tend to rent have been snapped up by former homeowners. The decline in ownership that resulted in a large increase in rentals has also driven up the price of those rentals. Rents are up 20% over the last four years.

By 2014, as stated before, due to supply and demand, renting is far more expensive than it used to be. In fancy Wall Street jargon, "Homeownership is more expensive because it is a factor of down payment." If that down payment is such an enormous factor, certainly one can see the advantage of the VA Home Loan Benefit. The VA buyer can purchase a house for *zero down!* Remove that down payment road block, and the odds return in your favor.

Sometimes people will compare and contrast the numbers and shake their heads at the results which suggest that owning a home is more costly than renting. Be careful to make sure you are not comparing apples with oranges. Sure a house can be more expensive...*you are most often buying more space!* No wonder the numbers run higher. The typical transition from being a renter to being a homeowner usually includes a jump or an increase in square footage. While it is not always the case, people tend to go from smaller rents to larger living spaces when they buy.

Now added to the growing list of advantages of buying a house, even in tough times, are the tax advantages. The real tax break is on the profit you make! If you sell a home and make money on it…as long as you buy a new home at the same price or greater then you don't have to pay capital gains tax on that home. When you reinvest you don't pay any taxes on it. (Other tax advantages may include the deductions of mortgage interest and property taxes. *(Disclaimer: We're not giving tax advice; please consult a tax professional for current tax code.)*

As we have discussed both sides of the rent vs. buy equation, with rare exception, we suggest you *buy* when you can afford to do so. With zero down, you can't really afford not to.

You may get to the point where it seems there are only obstacles in your way to owning a home. At SoCalVAHomes, we offer solutions to your frustrations and these roadblocks.

Should you rent or buy?

We can help you buy.

Will your VA Home Loan Benefit really help?

Yes.

As we said previously, our mortgage company, One Touching Lending, has been working with active military and Veterans since 9/11. A breakthrough occurred in 2011 as One Touch Lending was doing large volumes of refinances for VA homeowners. Our market of VA home buyers was silent for years due to higher home prices and the lack of higher VA loan limits – they were effectively locked out. As home prices declined from the peak in 2006 and

VA loan limits were raised, our market woke up! In 2008, VA home buyers began coming out from hiding! And in 2011, several thousand had now bought homes across California. Interest rates dropped like a rock in 2011 and created a refinance boom. This "boom" of VA refinance loan volume provided new insights into the market for me.

The sheer number of conversations that I had with hundreds of VA refinance clients over those many months was the catalyst to creating SoCalVAHomes. The conversations clearly demonstrated the problems that I later set out to solve! During that time, I had that "aha moment!" I came up with an idea that is revolutionary in the VA market. What if I were to purchase homes, renovate them to the specific needs of the veteran, and sell them to our clients for zero down, zero closing? An idea in a vacuum is just a concept, so we surveyed our own clients and prospective clients to gauge their reaction. Their response was more than positive. It was ecstatic! Here was a solution to a vexing problem.

While getting into a home for reduced prices (especially in a recession) was surprisingly good news, we saw something we believe to be wrong: the VA Home Loan Benefit was actually a liability. As the market moved dramatically from a buyer's market in 2008 to a seller's market in 2014, it became very difficult for VA buyers to compete with cash buyers because the housing inventory was so low. Reality can be harsh, and the reality here is that the market favors cash buyers and conventional buyers who can make huge down payments and large good faith deposits into escrow, securing their commitment to buy homes. By contrast, VA buyers are considered less desirable.

Typically, when someone uses their VA Home Loan Benefit in order to purchase a house with no money down, the marketplace tends not to be readily accepting of VA buyers. (Remember the VA Guaranty is not a guarantee that you will be able to buy a house, but rather that the U.S. Government promises to "insure" the lender against loss on a percentage of the loan should the buyer default). That fact that sellers don't favor VA buyers is an injustice (especially since the VA Guaranty was created as an honor and a leg-up for Veterans).

The reality is that sellers favor everyone except VA buyers! As we've written before in *The SoCalVAHomes.org story,* "a 'VA buyer' is traditionally the slowest, most restrictive, most expensive transaction for the seller, and the riskiest offer to accept with the worst odds of closing the transaction."

It was at this point that SARTRE, our real estate investment company, joined forces with One Touch Lending and created the concept of SoCalVAHomes and created the revolutionary DreamWeaver Home Purchase Process™. If the best homes were being purchased with cash offers, why not buy homes for cash then customize them ("add value") and sell them to VA clients for a small profit? Our revolutionary concept helps a client base we care about and support - active military and Veterans.

The Great Recession caused millions to lose their houses, forcing those who were previously homeowners to move into the rental market creating a "renter nation" (despite the aforementioned 65.4% of Americans who still own homes). That renter nation counter trend is being challenged by those who wish to and who can buy a home once again. In my opinion you are still better off buying a home. Some analysis concludes that buying a home is statistically 44.1% cheaper over time. It's a complex equation which compares factors like rising rental payments (that disappear into your landlord's pocket) vs. home ownership costs and financial benefits over time.

For assistance in making the decision to rent or buy, call us at 888-556-2018

Chapter 2: How to Buy a Lovely Home

The nuts, bolts, and key ingredients of a successful home purchase using your VA Home Loan Benefit.

As an active military service member or as a Veteran, you most likely have heard of the VA Home Loan Benefit and how it can help you to buy a house with no down payment.

The VA Home Loan Benefit dates back to 1944, when in support of American military personnel, Congress passed the Servicemen's Readjustment Act (more commonly known as the GI  Bill) to honor and help servicemen who've sacrificed for their nation. The Readjustment Act leveled the playing field for Veterans who wanted to purchase a home, but didn't have established credit and savings for a down payment because they were in active service.

The VA home loan is not a loan from the government. It is a loan from institutional lenders who are "VA approved." It centers around a Guaranty to the lender in the form of an insurance pool that assures that the government will pay 25% of the loan balance to the lender if the borrower defaults and the lender suffers a loss. The opportunity to get 100% financing on a house is the tip of the iceberg in terms of benefits; the financial protection of the benefit is immense.

All lenders, especially on a VA loan, have special considerations for service members who are deployed. As an example, imagine that a crisis breaks out in the Middle East or some other war-torn area and the service member is deployed overseas. There is often no time for him or her to get their finances together before returning to service. (By dropping everything and leaving home to serve, they may soon find their home in foreclosure, but the VA benefit offers protection against such a foreclosure). It is an incredible program that has helped over twenty million borrowers become homeowners since the program's inception during World War II.

Benefits

- 100% financing of the purchase price – no down payment.
- Lenient credit requirements.
- Reduced funding fee with a 5% or more down payment.
- Funding fee exemption for the disabled Veteran.
- An "assumable mortgage" (a mortgage that is transferred from seller to buyer.)
- The right to make prepayments without penalty.
- Forgiveness for temporary default due to borrower hardship via VA assistance.
- Closing costs negotiable – opportunity for nothing out of pocket to purchase a home.

Eligibility

- Veterans who've been honorably discharged.
- Active military, typically with 90 days of active service (depends on conflict served.)
- Un-remarried spouse of a military member whose death was a result of service or a service related disability.

- Spouse of a service member missing in action or a prisoner of war.

- Spouse who remarries after a certain age or date, as defined by the VA.

- Surviving spouses of certain disabled Veterans whose disability may not have been the cause of death.

- Other: Officers of National Oceanic & Atmospheric Administration, merchant seaman with World War II service, and others are also eligible. Contact the Department of Veterans Affairs for more information.

Generally speaking, when shopping for a mortgage loan, you will find four fundamental home loan categories that have both similarities and also major differences: conventional loans, government-backed loans: FHA and VA loans, and the "non-conforming loan."

A **conventional loan** is not guaranteed by the government, and thus requires a 20% down payment (or private mortgage insurance) and is typically harder to qualify for than a FHA or VA loan.

A **Federal Housing Administration** (FHA) loan is insured against default by the government, and is less difficult to qualify for than a conventional loan, but contains mortgage insurance that is commonly considered "expensive."

The **VA loan** has a 25% Guaranty, insuring the lender against default, created by the US Dept of Veteran's Affairs. It offers 100% financing, has more lenient qualification guidelines, and demands consideration if you qualify. Often, VA loans have better rates than conventional loans.

Non-Conforming loan. Many people who do not meet the financial criteria for a conforming loan consider a non-conforming loan. A conforming loan may be defined as "conforming" to a set of guidelines set forth by the government-sponsored enterprises: The Federal National Mortgage Association (FNMA) or the Federal Home Loan Mortgage Corporation (FHLMC)

Guidelines for a Conforming Loan

- Loan amount maximum: currently $417,000; higher loan limits are available for high cost counties.

- Loan-to-value ratio (LTV): This is the loan amount divided by the total value of the property. Common requirements don't allow loan amounts to exceed 80% of the value of the home unless some sort of mortgage insurance component is coupled with the new loan.

- Debt-to-income ratio (DTI) considers your monthly debt payments. If your monthly expenditures are more than 45% of your pre-tax income, you may have to consider a non-conforming loan. Some conforming loans can be approved with debt ratios as high as 60%. Many "compensating factors" and or advantageous circumstances would exist.

- Credit Score and history. Borrowers are expected to have a Fair Isaac Credit Risk score of 620-640 or greater. Exceptions may apply.

- Documentation requirements: EVERYTHING is needed! Income, assets, and employment history.

Jumbo Loans are simply loans that are too large to fit into conforming loan amount guidelines. Whether you are using a conventional loan, an FHA loan, or your VA loan to finance the property, there are three things that are common to all financing:

- Income
- Equity, Reserves (not required with VA loans)
- Credit

Income

Lenders consider how much you make and whether you are employed or self-employed. Lenders use net income (not gross income) from your tax returns if you are self-employed. Thus, many self-employed people think they make a lot money, but by the time they file their tax returns, they often don't qualify for a mortgage. They don't have a large net income relative to their gross income, and that's a really common element of angst and anxiety for folks who think they can buy, but then find out they really can't. Additionally, those who are employed and deduct a large amount of "unreimbursed employee expenses" can be disappointed when an underwriter deducts those expenses from their wage income.

Equity

Equity can be described as a down payment and/or your reserves. (Reserves are cash-in-the bank, a retirement account, CDs, or any other liquid assets.) The fact that no down payment is required and no reserves are required is a big advantage for those using their VA benefit. That's not the case with any other loan.

In a transaction where closing costs are negotiated, closing costs can be paid for by the lender or the seller, and the net result to a VA buyer could be zero down and zero closing! That is a *huge* benefit for a client who typically hasn't saved a lot of money for a down payment.

Credit

Credit is the last thing that all loan underwriting guidelines have in common. Borrowers must meet minimum credit requirements. Conventional loans have the most stringent credit requirements. FHA and VA loans have the least stringent credit requirements.

VA financing allows for **credit risk scores** of 500 (as is the case with FHA as well). However, if credit scores are below 620, a "make sense" approach is utilized when reviewing loan applications. If you are a conventional buyer, underwriters would really prefer 680 or better. These are common Fair Isaac Credit Risk scores needed for these types of loans. Some variations can apply. The **VA loan and FHA loans** are definitely the most lenient.

Debt Ratios

What are Debt Ratios? **Debt-to-Income Ratios** measure how much of your monthly income goes toward repaying your monthly debts.

Income (as previously defined) is the "denominator" in the computation of the ratio. The "numerator" begins with your house payment which is comprised of principal and interest, plus your real estate taxes, your homeowner's insurance and any homeowner's association fees. That's your total mortgage payment as a VA buyer. Taxes and insurance are always required to be impounded – collected as part of the payment in an escrow account under your name. So the lender will be collecting 1/12 of your property taxes on a monthly basis and 1/12 of your annual homeowner insurance on a monthly basis for each mortgage payment.

In addition to the total housing payment, a car payment and credit cards are added to the equation. All these payments are summed up to total "the numerator" - your total housing expense plus all your other monthly obligations. Divide the sum by your gross income (or your net income if you are self-employed,) and the result is your **Debt Ratio**. Lenders like to see that debt ratio at 41% or less. There's a limit to how much you can borrow or qualify for based on your income. That 41% ratio can be very flexible if other *compensating factors* are present.

Automated Underwriting Result vs Manual Underwriting

There are computer programs in the mortgage industry that utilize all of your data - your credit risk scores, credit profile, income, and asset information. These programs digest all the data and render a decision to "approve" the loan or to refer the decision to a real human for a manual review. When the computer program approves the loan file (using bonafide, accurate borrower information,) the loan underwriting and approval can be more lenient. Higher debt ratios can then be achieved, and less documentation is necessary to collect. When the computer does *not* approve the loan file, it refers the loan for manual underwriting. This is because the borrower data represents a marginal decision, and a more careful evaluation of the borrower's qualifications is necessary (in the computer program's infinite wisdom.) If a manual underwrite is the case, higher debt ratios typically are not allowed. Compensating factors that can influence all underwriting can be:

- Having lots of reserves - money in the bank.
- Long duration with one employer.
- Having excellent credit.

Those factors will allow the underwriters to be more liberal in terms of the debt ratios.

In regard to an expanded discussion regarding **Credit Scores** and your credit profile, I have written about the subject in a different chapter (see Chapter 16: Why You Shouldn't Cry Over Your Credit.) A solid rule of thumb remains that it is better to have great credit than average credit, but average credit is all you need to buy a home using your VA Home Loan Benefit! However, improving your credit is always a good idea.

SoCalVAHomes uses three very powerful, proprietary programs to combat the disadvantages and frustrations that VA home buyers can experience when attempting to buy a home. For further information, call SoCalVAHomes at 888-556-2018 or visit socalvahomes.org

Chapter 3: "Your Documents, Please!"

How to get your Certificate of Eligibility and Why ALL this documentation is so important to using your VA Home Loan Benefit.

Active military and Veterans often ask our staff, "How do I get my Certificate of Eligibility?" And then, when we get into the actual processing of their VA home loan, they ask, "Why do I have to provide *all of this documentation for a VA loan?*"

Yes...all the requests for documents and paperwork can be a little challenging, *but the result is always worth it*, and tens of millions of VA borrowers before you have traveled this path! Listed below is some of the required documentation that needs to be provided when you utilize your VA Home Loan Benefit.

To apply for and fund a VA home loan, an underwriter will need to review your Certificate of Eligibility (COE). Your Certificate of Eligibility will provide the current status of your VA loan benefit. If you are fully "entitled" to your benefit, then it is unencumbered, meaning your benefit is available to its maximum. If you have previously used all of your entitlement and that loan is yet to be paid off, then your entitlement is zero and simply unavailable. Your Certificate of Eligibility will reflect that encumbrance or usage. If you did not utilize your benefit to its

maximum, and it is yet to be paid off, your Certificate of Eligibility will reflect that partially encumbered entitlement. In this case, you may take advantage of the remainder of your entitlement, but your entitlement won't get restored to 100% until the previous loan is paid off.

If you're not on active duty, you'll also need your Certificate of Release from Active Duty (DD Form 214.) Your DD214 will need to demonstrate your Character of Service as Honorable, essentially an Honorable Discharge, and your DD214 will typically need to demonstrate 90 days or more of active service. Surviving spouses and others may also qualify for this benefit. According to the VA, if you fall into the following groups, you may also qualify for eligibility:

- Certain U.S. citizens who served in the armed forces of a government allied with the United States in World War II.

- Individuals with service as members in certain organizations, such as Public Health Service officers, cadets at the United States Military, Air Force or Coast Guard Academy, midshipmen at the United States Naval Academy, officers of National Oceanic & Atmospheric Administration, merchant seaman with World War II service, and others.

According to the VA, "If you do not meet the minimum service requirements, you may still be eligible if you were discharged due to (1) hardship, (2) the convenience of the government, (3) reduction-in-force, (4) certain medical conditions, or (5) a service-connected disability." You can obtain your Certificate of Eligibility simply by going online at www.ebenefitsVA.gov. Getting a Certificate of Eligibility is primarily an online activity. However, SoCalVAHomes performs this process and obtains COEs for clients regularly as a courtesy.

Preparing for the Inquisition!

The "requests for documentation" have just begun! For many people, the sheer volume of required documentation can be a little daunting. You'll be asked for such things as your award letter for  your disability payments (if applicable) and any annual increases on that award. Next, be prepared with bank statements showing the automatic deposit of your disability payments. Expect the same type of requests for military retirement and social security with both the award letter and bank statements showing deposits. With regard to your bank statements, you may be asked to explain "large" deposits! A large deposit can be anything in their opinion. This questioning is all at the underwriter's discretion.

Why do underwriters ask you about these deposits? One of the main reasons, and it's often surprising to people, is anti-money-laundering concerns. It's standard practice for criminals to obtain money illegally, try to "wash it" or launder it somehow, and then attempt to get it into a bank, and then turn it into a down payment on a piece of property! As deceitful as that concept might sound to the legitimate buyer, it's a protection element aimed at helping those people who are doing the right thing.

The bottom line is anti-money-laundering laws and the CFPB (Consumer Finance Protection Bureau) have created a rigorous environment to operate and lend since the financial crisis of 2008. There have always been stringent underwriting requirements for VA home loans guaranteed by the Department of Veterans Affairs, but the financial crisis hasn't made it easier for our VA borrowers when applying for a loan.

When applying for a VA loan, you may experience form requests for childcare statements, requests for nearest living relative statements, an alive-and-well letter from a commanding officer, verification of VA benefits forms, and letters of explanation for anything that seems outside the norm. This long laundry list of things can seem exhausting. It's all intended for the lender to package the loan correctly to obtain the "VA Loan Guaranty." A VA loan has to be documented per a specific set of guidelines to obtain that VA Loan Guaranty for the lender. Without the Guaranty from the VA, the lender can't sell the loan, and the mechanism for the availability of 100% financing for YOUR benefit fails. This is why lots of documentation is necessary. Try not to get frustrated with the process. Instead, be prepared for it, and enjoy the ride as you purchase your new home!

If you would like assistance with obtaining your Certificate of Eligibility and understanding VA loan documentation, call SoCalVAHomes at 888-556-2018.

Chapter 4: What You Should Know About The Gatekeeper

The VA Appraiser and the VA Appraisal. The pros and cons of the VA Escape Clause, VA Amendatory Clause and the Tidewater Initiative

If you are an active military member or a Veteran looking to become a homeowner, you need to know about the advantages and disadvantages of VA appraisals. When you are in the midst of processing a VA loan, hopefully you'll find out that the VA appraiser is really on your side, but there are some drawbacks that you need to know about.

As previously mentioned, VA offers are not the first choice for sellers who would prefer cash and conventional buyers. One reason for this preference is the VA appraiser is often stringent in their opinions of the property because they're being protective of YOU. But there are advantages and  disadvantages with that VA appraisal, depending on your view point. The appraiser can be conservative, rigid, and even slow to complete. This can cause delays in the purchasing of the property. It can even crush transactions, primarily due to the final value placed on the home and placed on the appraisal document.

Let's take an example, one that shows an advantage and disadvantage of a VA appraisal in the same attempted transaction. VA appraisals and the corresponding value of the home can come in lower than the negotiated purchase price. For example, let's say that a buyer and seller agree on a selling price of $400,000 for the house. Then the VA appraiser does the inspection, looks at comparable sales of the property, finds issues, and then finally puts a value of $385,000 on it. Thankfully for the VA buyer, part of the required VA documentation in the transaction is the VA amendatory clause or "escape clause." This protects the VA buyer because the seller cannot force the buyer to purchase the property at the contract purchase price of $400,000. In this circumstance, this buyer will have an option to pay cash for the difference in the contract price of $400,000 and the appraised value of $385,000. The buyer and seller may also entirely renegotiate the price, or the buyer may choose to "escape" the transaction and cancel altogether without any recourse from the seller. That protective measure is certainly an advantage for the VA buyer so the buyer is not paying more than the property is actually worth (in the opinion of the VA appraiser.)

One perceived disadvantage could be that the VA appraiser is being too conservative (even "picky"). For example, one of my clients had a recent experience with a picky appraiser. An entry walkway had a slight rise on a portion of it, and the concrete had some cracks in it. The appraiser called it a safety hazard, whereas most people's more moderate opinion would be that it was just a small, correctable problem. The appraiser was just doing his job, but the walkway had to be repaired prior to closing. It's a typical example demonstrating that the VA appraisal can pose both advantages and disadvantages, depending on your view.

When the VA appraiser makes a determination in the buyer's favor, the VA Amendatory Escape Clause is activated. This escape clause is a non-negotiable clause required by real estate law. The definition of the actual escape clause is as follows:

"It is expressly agreed that notwithstanding any other provision of this contract, the purchaser shall not incur any penalty by forfeiture of earnest money or otherwise be obligated to complete the purchase of the property described herein if the contract price or costs exceeds the reasonable value of the property established by the Department of Veterans' Affairs," (e.g. the VA appraiser). In other words, "Buyer, here's your out."

The escape clause can certainly be perceived as a disadvantage to the seller, creating some reservation and resistance to accepting a VA offer. With the previous example of the property sold for $400,000, let's say they appraiser declares the value to be $385,000. The VA won't guarantee the loan amount in excess of $385,000. What if the buyer believes that the property is definitely worth more than $385,000 and is willing to pay for the difference?

The second part of the clause actually allows for the buyer to pay the difference. It's an infrequent experience but not an uncommon experience, especially in a competitive "seller's market" where there are many more buyers than there are sellers. Buyers may be more willing to stretch themselves and pay higher prices even though the appraisers don't think that the property is worth it. This puts the buyer and seller in a position to renegotiate. Let's say, in the example of the difference between $400,000 and $385,000, that the buyer and seller split the difference and renegotiate the contract price at $392,500, and they both concede $7500. In that instance, the buyer would contribute the $7500 and conclude the transaction.

In this manner, the VA Escape Clause really is a great protective measure. It acts as a conservative counterbalance. However, when the conservative VA appraised value gets attached to the appraisal, that result can create havoc in the midst of two motivated buyers and sellers! The seller could easily decide the VA appraiser is too conservative, and decide to sell the property to somebody else.

In our experience, the VA Escape Clause tends to lean as a benefit to the buyer. The value difference between the contract price and the appraised value is often minimal. And frankly, the only leverage that the common VA offer has over its competition in a hot market is to offer the highest price. That may entice the seller to accept the VA offer when the seller is just "letting the market dictate what the home is worth." When the VA appraiser comes back with a lower value, it's not a tremendous shock to the seller because they accepted the offer with the highest price anyway. The next step in the transaction becomes a renegotiation at a lower price, which can favor our buyer, if they have the cash to pay the difference between the new price and the appraised value.

For assistance in finding properties that fit within appraisal guidelines and making a VA offer to purchase, let SoCalVAHomes help. Call us at 888-556-2018.

Chapter 5: "No Mello Roos, and Hold the HOA Please!"

The pros and cons of HOAs (Home Owner Associations,) Mello Roos "taxes"and should you buy a condo using your VA Home Loan Benefit?

Home Owners Associations or "HOA"s are the governing body that oversees a "community" of housing units, whether they are condominiums, co-operatives or single family residences. The  HOAs are typically responsible for "managing" the property management company that cares for common areas which can include landscaping, buildings and recreational facilities too. The HOAs operate like a government for the community as they set and adjust policies and manage budgets for community expenses. As a "VA home buyer" using your VA home loan benefit, you must determine whether you want to own a property that has a HOA. Ownership of a condominium will include the governance of and your payments to an HOA.

Let's talk about the possibility of buying a condo using your VA Home Loan Benefit. First, you have to make sure that you can actually obtain VA financing on the condo that is managed by an HOA. Condominium projects must apply for and obtain an approval from the Department of Veterans Affairs. The VA doesn't automatically assume that the real estate developer and the HOA have their act together! If you google "VA condo search," you'll reach the VA portal. Place the project name as it is officially known in the search bar and the portal will tell you whether it's "VA approved" and whether you're going to have any challenges in terms of getting a VA home loan on that property. If it's a single-family residence and not "parceled" in any way as a condo by the original developer, you're not going to have any problem with the property itself. You won't need it to be "VA approved." There might be problems with the actual collateral or condition of the property, but that's a different issue.

Some condos are not "VA approved" because the builder doesn't see the cost of obtaining the VA approval as a worthwhile expense. If the VA is going to allow a loan on a property within a "community" built by a real estate developer, the VA has many property standards and HOA standards that must be met. The builder may see enough volume of conventional home buyers buying their units, so they simply won't bother with the VA approval process. During "The Financial Crisis," many condos were forced into foreclosure, resulting in a dramatic reduction of revenue from the owner's monthly payments to the HOA. In many projects, a large percentage of the total number of units was foreclosed upon. In managing  their HOA budget, the managers didn't expect a huge reduction to their income from HOA fees, and they had to make adjustments. To continue to provide services to those home owners still in the community, and to project and maintain the HOA budget, managers had to raise prices and increase the HOA fees. This happened all across Southern California and all across the country. In order to financially resurrect entire communities managed by HOAs, managers had to raise prices to match budgets. In the midst of all that, there were a lot of investors who purchased these properties and paid cash. You might perceive that as beneficial as the HOA revenues began to climb again. However, this event magnified an already difficult problem in these communities still suffering from HOA budgeting issues. The larger concentration of investor owned units created the following financing problems.

Here is the big problem: FHA is the primary source of financing for most borrowers who consider purchasing a condo. This is primarily because of the lower prices associated with condos. Lower prices mean smaller down payments and that attracts FHA borrowers. FHA, and conventional financing, requires a minimum number of owner-occupied units in relationship to investor-owned units. Without meeting this minimum, no loan approval will be granted. **The number of investor owned units in many projects increased dramatically when these foreclosed units became available and were purchased for cash at deeply discounted prices.**

FHA also requires a minimum amount of reserves in the HOA budget. They want to prevent the HOA from poorly running the project and thereby deteriorating property values which would increase their risk of loss on a foreclosure. If the HOA loses lots of income resulting from foreclosures, they are less likely to properly budget maintenance projects such as road re-surfacing, exterior painting, landscape, amenities maintenance, etc. The bottom line is that **foreclosures really challenge HOA budgets, which reduces reserves below FHA minimum requirements,** creating a "liquidity crisis."

Liquidity in this case can be defined as the owner's ability to easily sell their home (at a reasonable price) while the buyer facilitates the other end of the transaction by using traditional financing, likely FHA. These properties can't be bought and sold if there is not financing, typically FHA financing. And FHA financing wasn't going to happen unless the proper reserves were in the HOA budget, and often, hundreds of thousands of dollars in reserve are needed in the HOA budget. These communities needed enough cash buyers to come in, buy, and to occupy, thereby correcting the "owner occupancy ratio."

Communities then began raising monthly dues, and the homeowners who were barely making it defaulted on the higher HOA fees, which added to the foreclosures. **Ultimately, the monthly HOA fees in these communities experienced dramatic increases**. With appropriate budgeting, the reserve requirements and owner-occupancy ratios were re-aligned by market forces to create "liquidity" again. At that point, financing options resurfaced. However, HOA fees are now, by and large, MUCH higher than before 2008. So you now have to ask yourself, "What am I getting for my $250-$500 a month HOA fee?" On the high end, you might be able to take advantage of clubhouses and community pools, sometimes multiple community pools, tennis courts, and great landscaping. In less attractive projects, with lower HOA fees, you may only get a parking lot and a carport. As a potential buyer, you'll have to evaluate the merits of the benefits offered in the community vs. the HOA fees.

All homeowners' associations have CCRs, which stand for Conditions, Covenants, and Restrictions. There may be "by laws" for the project too. These are the documents guiding the governing body, usually the Board of Directors of the HOA, and the home owners. The board is typically comprised of the homeowners themselves. Sometimes there may be an external property management company that sits on the board or is directed by the board to carry out maintenance objectives, etc. The board makes decisions regarding things like what color you can paint your house or what trees to plant in common areas. Often they are good decisions, but you may not always agree with them. They are essentially telling you what you can do and what you can't do, and most people would prefer that nobody tells them what to do! In properties that have HOAs, you can get annoying neighbors who complain about all sorts of stuff! They often wage little micropolitical struggles within the board or against specific board members, especially during elections. It can get strange, and you won't know it before you buy in that community.

Concerning appreciation and depreciation of the property value, historical data suggests that condos are going to be the last to appreciate and the first to depreciate. Be cautious if you're thinking that you'll definitely make money on such a property purchase. Don't PLAN on it, but instead be grateful if and when it occurs. You want to be cautious about expectations of making money on real estate. Make your decisions based on pride of ownership, affordability, and tax consequences, before you anticipate profit.

Also, you really want to be concerned about affordability as it relates to how that monthly HOA fee factors in your affordability picture. Certainly the underwriter's conclusion about your affordability picture should be concerning as they are thinking the same thing you are - can you afford all this? As we look at HOA fees in Southern California and all communities, they are not insignificant anymore. There might have been a time we could ignore them, but that's not the case today. There's a "value proposition," and there are affordability concerns that you have to measure, as you make your purchase decisions. As an hypothetical example, let's say you go out in the marketplace and you find a $350,000 condo with a $350/month HOA fee. When you factor in your affordability, contrast that potential condo purchase with a $390,000 single-family residence with no HOA fee. Your overall payments will be the same. Perhaps the single family home has more potential for appreciation. So, as it relates to your property search, you may discover potential communities where you're going to look at a condo and other locations where you'll decide you don't see the value. You have to weigh all that when making your decision. Think seriously about how specific HOAs factor into your decision.

Mello Roos "Taxes"

Mello Roos "taxes" are actually bond payments. When new communities are being built without the supporting tax

infrastructure to finance the "build out" of the city, the city has to issue a Mello Roos bond to pay for the new infrastructure such as roads and schools. These municipal bonds are "floated" or issued by investment bankers to the investment community. Investors buy the bonds, and the sales proceeds, or money received from the issuance of the bonds, stacks up in a fund. The developers use those funds to develop the entire communities' infrastructure. They build the middle school, the grammar school, the high school, and all the roads, etc.

In a Mello Roos tax district, each homeowner's property tax assessment includes the Mello Roos payments to pay their portion of the bond payment. All the homeowner's payments are aggregated together to make the total bond payment to the investors, typically for a term of twenty to twenty five years. At the end of the term, the investors have received their principal and interest.

We don't know if the IRS has ever challenged the definition of "property taxes" vs. "bond payments," but everybody we know, including all of our CPAs, endorses deducting the Mello Roos payments as a tax-deductible expense. *(Again, we are not offering tax advice. Please consult your CPA or tax professional regarding this issue.)*

Is a Mello Roos "tax" good or is it bad? It depends on your perception. It's going to increase your property taxes, typically double what other homeowner's may pay. This makes owning your property more expensive. However, you're going to get a lot for that! Typically you're getting a brand new community infrastructure. A lot of these communities build great parks, sports programs, new facilities, new schools and classrooms. The advantage of the Mello Roos tax is that you can see what it pays for - great new schools, new roads, etc. The disadvantage is that it is costly. And it's coming out of your taxes. And that's going to affect your *affordability.*

You should be comparing the Mello Roos community over here vs. the non- Mello Roos community across town. What are the affordability disadvantages compared to the "value" advantages. Additionally, there's certainly going to be some consideration regarding property values as these Mello Roos taxes mature and the bond payments terminate. Imagine you are buying a property where your tax base is currently 2-1/2%. But three years from now, when the bond payments to the investors conclude, that tax base is going to be 1%. What do you think that's going to do to property values? Obviously the home will be more affordable, so buyers will view that as a benefit and pay for it. Demand increases appreciation!

For assistance in finding the right community and the right property for you, let SoCalVAHomes help. Call 888-556-2018.

Chapter 6: Poor-Looking Properties Produce Problems!

Financing with your VA Home Loan Benefit is hard with

these property condition stumbling blocks

By learning what property condition challenges will prevent your financing, you'll learn how to be successful when you want to buy a house with your VA Home Loan Benefit. When you are purchasing a property, hopefully you are working with a qualified real estate professional and a home inspector. The property will need to be inspected by a VA certified appraiser. VA appraisers adhere to very strict guidelines. This is where the challenges occur.

Outside of simple "project approval" issues, there are a variety of property condition issues discussed in this chapter that will sabotage a purchase financed by a VA home loan. Remember to consider these concerns as buyer protection and *self*-protection! The VA appraiser completes an inspection for the purposes of arriving at a home's value. That inspection can be very helpful with regard to understanding specific property deficiencies, if any exist. A professional home inspector's conclusions will likely provide a more in depth report regarding the condition of a home as well. A good home inspector will also review their inspection findings with you. Both are great tools for your protection.

Property Conditions and Concerns

Here is a partial list of possible repairs to be aware of:

- Termites: There may be problems with wood-destroying pests that have infested the property. A qualified termite inspector needs to come in, and ultimately, a  termite certification or clearance needs to be provided for final underwriting approval in VA financing. Repairs are typically negotiable regarding who's going to pay for them. Often, it's the seller, but it is negotiable.

- Slab cracks. Ouch! They may need repair.

- Roof: The roof is something that you always want to be concerned about, especially in areas with significant amounts of rain, and where the house has old asphalt shingles. You can repair the roof and add a new layer of shingles for a total of three layers before all of it needs to be excised off the roof, and you need a brand new roof.

- Solar energy is a big advantage for a lot of our clients. Almost every homeowner can reduce their energy bill by using solar panels. It's economically attractive in most cases. If you have your heart set on solar, you're really going to want to pay attention to the roof inspection as it relates to any potential repairs or structural issues. You can get a specialty roof inspector, as opposed to an inspector who's going to inspect the entire property including the slab and the "mechanicals" - (electrical, plumbing, et. al.).

- Slope: In California, there's a lot of slope! For older properties, drainage can be something that ends up on the deferred maintenance list, and you do not want rainwater draining toward/into the property. This is an issue that you need to be concerned about.
- Water heaters always need to be strapped correctly. That's building code.
- Carbon monoxide detectors are required by law. They are easy to install and are inexpensive. You can purchase one for as little as $30, but carbon monoxide detectors are priceless because they can save your life.
- Gas water heaters and gas stoves, by law, have to have flex lines.
- Electrical systems are a complex issue. The Ground Fault Interrupter or GFI switch is required to be six feet from any water source. There are potential safety hazards with old electrical plugs that aren't grounded and old electrical systems in general.
- Mold
- Asbestos
- Lead-based paint was banned in 1978, but can still exist.
- Underground storage tanks, including septic tanks are often still used. Check and see if they are obsolete and need to be updated or removed.
- Tanks in the wrong places, such as inappropriately parked in the

driveway!…interesting picture, huh? Couldn't help it! ☺

For assistance with determining if a specific property will ultimately qualify for VA financing, let SoCalVAHomes help. Call us at 888-556-2018.

Chapter 7: How to Buy a BIGGER Lovely Home!

Important tactics to use when movin' up and buying a bigger home using your VA Home Loan Benefit. How to use private lending to your advantage.

I'm sure you know that as active military or as a Veteran, you can sell your home and buy a bigger home *and use your VA Home Loan Benefit for financing a second time.* Putting all the moving parts together to accomplish this goal can be an overwhelming

task. Let's talk about all the mechanics – all the elements you must consider and implement to accomplish your goals.

Start by asking yourself, do you need to do anything to your current home to sell it? Many people feel like they do. Some absolutely need to, and some do not, depending on whether the home has recently been fully upgraded.

At SoCalVAHomes, we've certainly sold our fair share of homes over the years (well over a thousand,) and some of those homes were ready to put on the market from day one. Having a market-ready house is unusual – a bit of a rarity. It's a good idea to ask someone who's qualified and knows the market about what needs to be done to the home to allow it to compete for a buyer's attention. In a "hot market" with little supply, maybe you don't have to do a thing to your home. If there are upgrades that need to be done, ask yourself if you can pay cash for the improvements or if you need to finance them? Of course your answer is a result of the cost of the upgrades and how much you can afford to spend.

If you need cash to make those home improvements, you might want to take a look at a **VA cash-out loan**. But be careful. You only want to consider a VA cash-out loan if you can eliminate all the costs. Why? Because you're going to sell the home, and you don't want to incur a higher loan balance if you can avoid it. How do you eliminate the costs? You'll need to accept a higher than "market rate," a "premium rate," where the lender pays all the closing costs. It would help if you were exempt from the funding fee (by currently receiving disability benefits) when using a VA cash-out refinance to pay for your improvements to get the property ready for sale. That's a big undertaking and it is also time consuming. To get the cash from a refinance takes 30 to 60 days, and it will take another 30 to 60 days, or longer, to do all the needed improvements.

As an option for a smaller makeover, you might consider a home equity line of credit. The home equity line of credit is typically the lower-cost option of any financing. You should be able to obtain a home equity line of credit for free at most of the major banks and credit unions. If you can't qualify for the home equity line, usually that's a matter of lack of equity. Of course you can think about installment payments to a home improvement finance company, but try to stay away from finance companies. They usually have very high rates and fees. They also can construct financing contracts which require all the interest, which would be charged in the contract's entirety, be paid at payoff – essentially a prepayment fee.

Private Lending to Finance Upgrades

Our company SoCalVAHomes is a unique company that does things other companies do not or can not do. We offer private lending to select clients. This is a loan out of our pocket, from our coffers to you, as a courtesy above all else. We can use our money to prepare your property for sale. Under such a circumstance, we would take on the listing, market the property for sale, and help you achieve your purchase goals as well. We consider private loans to clients for moderate sums in the range of less than $50,000. Why is it a "courtesy" to put so much of our cash out on the line? We take risks that no other company would, for returns on our capital that investors would laugh at and call us foolish! However, in this circumstance, we want to make sure that we're doing the right things to make your property marketable. We must oversee all aspects of property grooming, because again, we might be taking some extraordinary risks with our capital that others who lend money would consider just plain foolish!

Again, no one else would ever make such a private loan. We might, because we know you as a client, know your objectives, know the house, and we know what the house is going to sell for. We can guess the worst-case scenarios regarding the time it will take to sell your property and at what price. So literally, we're willing to make our own funds available for you to spruce up your property, if you can't find other adequate financing to accomplish the things necessary to sell the home.

The Moving Parts to Moving Up

When moving up to a larger home, you'll probably have to put the cart before the horse, which means getting qualified for that new home purchase first. And getting qualified means that there are number of things that need to be examined, primarily, equity, credit, income, and VA loan limits. Here's a quick overview:

Equity is the amount that you'll put down, if any, on the new home. Typical move-up buyers sell their current home, and then they receive the net cash proceeds as funds available for a down payment on the next home. In this circumstance, the buyer has a choice to make. If 100% financing is available (to the loan amount desired), should they use these funds for their home purchase? At the time of this writing, rates are extraordinarily inexpensive. There are VA jumbo rates (amounts greater than $417,000) lower than 4.00%! I advocate borrowing more at cheap rates, not less, but I also advocate realistic budgeting, living within your means, and optimizing the opportunity costs of your cash. For example, if you can get $100,000 in net proceeds from your sale, and you don't need all that for your down payment, and you're wondering what to do with it, you might want to consider *investing* $75,000 from the sale and using $25,000 for the down payment. You don't have to take all the net proceeds from the sale of your home and commit it to the new purchase. And I encourage you to seriously consider whether you should or should not be doing that. Therefore, as it relates to qualifying for the new home, you'll want to examine the equity component. Is making a down payment necessary or unnecessary to accomplish your goals?

Credit: Take a new look at your "mortgage credit report" with three "mortgage" scores. Don't gage your credit entirely by viewing "consumer" scores, especially not just one score! Make sure that your credit allows you to qualify for the financing you'll need to accomplish your goals.

Income: Have a qualified VA loan professional review your income and debt ratios to determine your highest loan amount you can qualify for. Get pre-approved for your new purchase. This process must consider the inclusion of your current housing expenses if you don't intend to sell your current home.

Loan limits: Currently, there are "high-cost" loan limits in excess of $417,000 that allow you to finance 100% of the purchase price in more expensive markets. But because these loan limits are ever changing, consult your loan professional for current high-cost county limits to determine if those high-cost county limits do or don't adequately provide enough financing for your maximum purchase price. If the loan limit falls short in any county, the VA will require that you contribute a 25% down payment between the purchase price of the property and the loan limit. As an example, let's just say the loan limit is $500,000 and you want to buy a $600,000 house. You could get a $575,000 loan because you only have to cover 25% of the difference between the $600,000 purchase price and the $500,000 loan limit. That 25% contribution to cover the difference between the loan limit and the purchase price is a huge advantage as compared to conventional down payments! We have buyers that are buying six, seven, eight hundred thousand dollar homes and only putting down $25,000 - $50,000, literally, because the high-cost loan limits are so high!

So…first determine that:

- You can sell your home at the right price and yield an acceptable amount in net proceeds.
- Your income and credit all are acceptable, qualifying you for your desired loan amount.
- The loan limits exist to allow you to finance the new loan amount you want...

You've now taken all the critical steps to prepare yourself for your new purchase goal. You're now ready to move up and buy a bigger home!

Your VA Entitlement

Your VA Entitlement must be in order. Selling your home which was financed using your VA Home Loan Benefit will restore your VA entitlement back to its maximum benefit. If you've used only a portion of your VA entitlement on your current home, and you don't intend on selling that home, then you have some math homework to do! Your VA entitlement will remain "encumbered" by your current loan. Consult a qualified VA mortgage professional to ensure the remaining entitlement is going to be enough to accomplish your goal. Calculating your remaining "unencumbered" entitlement and the resulting potential loan amount can be some tricky math, especially when a down payment is involved.

Coming Full Circle: Ready To Sell

Once you get all those qualifying pieces together and have made sure the mechanics and the logistics work, then you have to learn what kind of "market" you are currently in. You also need to know what kind of market conditions exist in your new target location. Is it balanced? Soft? Hot? Are there lots of homes for sale (more than a six month supply?) What's really going on? What's it going to take to sell your house and buy another?

The ideal strategy is to sell your home first and be flexible about the timing and circumstances of your move to your ultimate destination. Why is that ideal? That might sound like anything but ideal! Yet, from a negotiating standpoint, selling first and being patient on your purchase produces the optimal results in most markets.

Let's say you plan to sell your house and it's in the condition  you think it ought to be in to sell, but you haven't listed it yet. And low and behold, you find a new house you'd like to make an offer on! Now, you're about to engage in two transactions at once - the purchase of the new home and the sale of your current home. If you're trying to do two transactions at once - buying first and trying to sell second, you're coming from a weaker negotiating position on both transactions-- you don't want to do that!

In this scenario, you'll likely make a ***contingent offer*** to purchase the new home. And the seller may have multiple offers, so they'll balk at your "VA contingent offer to purchase." No seller is going to give you the time of day in anything but the "softest" of all real estate markets – a market where few buyers exist and many sellers. Why? Because sellers (and the realtors) want buyers who are prepared to close ASAP! Sellers view the home that you have to sell first as your anchor, holding you back from closing. Agents will also caution their sellers regarding all the other drawbacks associated with a VA transaction.   Again, these may include stringent appraisals, slower closing time frames, much smaller good faith deposits, etc. Most sellers don't even want to bother with a VA contingent offer.

In this circumstance, when you make an offer on that house you really want, you're only *REAL leverage* is price. You'll be inclined to pay a higher price in an effort to make your VA offer stand out. Then, if you *have to sell your home* in order to buy, you'll be more inclined to accept less on the home you're selling. No one wants to take less on the home they're selling and pay more for the home they're buying. Naturally, you want to do just the opposite.

So, how do you approach your "move UP" in the most strategic manner? ***You accomplish your home improvements, list, and sell your home first.*** With this sequence, you're in the strongest negotiating position when you're selling your home, because in the eyes of your buyer, you don't HAVE to sell! Then, when your current home is sold AND CLOSED (and hopefully a sizable down payment in the bank,) you'll make your strongest offer to purchase, not a contingent offer. With this strategy, you'll be in the most advantageous position, putting your best foot forward in both transactions. Yes, I know it can be a logistics hassle - storage, temporary housing,  two moves, not one - but it can definitely be worth the financial benefits.

Here's a strategy tip! A good qualified real estate sales professional is going to describe an advantage called a "**rent back**." That means selling your current home, closing the sale, and then staying in the home for, say, another 30-60 days, essentially renting the home from the new buyer. You're going to get fewer buyers who are interested in longer rent-backs, but the fact that you can stay in your home gives you the ability to bridge the gap between the sale of your home and the purchase of the next home. This is a great way to embark on the above strategy. The ultimate timing of the closing of the new purchase and moving out of your old home may not be perfect, but it's possible. And it's more effective than not attempting the "rent back" at all. Make sure that you ask your real estate professional about a rent back, and how that could work to your advantage when you're selling your home and moving up to the next one.

If you truly can't sell your house first, there are two scenarios where buying your new home first and then selling your current home might work. This may be logistically more pleasing to you and your family. These scenarios may work in a super-hot seller's market where you own a very attractive property. Because you're a VA buyer and don't need a down payment, you can sometimes afford to pay a little bit more than other buyers (who need to make a down payment) can afford to pay. It's a case by case scenario, but when VA offers are accepted, I can almost guarantee it's because they were offering the highest price. Because there are so many disadvantages, as a seller, when accepting a VA offer, the seller may tolerate the disadvantages because they wish to support a Veteran who served. But the bottom line is, the seller wants the highest price. **That's typically why they accept a VA offer**. If you're in that rare position where your VA offer is accepted on your purchase, and you've got a current home that's really attractive, in great condition, and can sell fast because it's a seller's market, go back and list your property at the right price. You can probably get it in escrow to sell within a week. That's one scenario where it may actually work for you.

The other scenario is a bit like waving a magic wand! SoCalVAHomes has developed and utilizes a proprietary purchase process called The Dreamweaver Home Purchase. In this circumstance, we actually buy a home (to renovate) for you, by paying cash to the seller. Obviously this is a "non-contingent" offer to purchase – it's a CASH offer on your behalf. We then close on the home and renovate it to your CUSTOM specifications. You then buy the home from us for zero down and zero closing costs using your VA Home Loan Benefit. In this scenario, you are afforded the luxury of time and control, as we assist in the sale of your current home. This scenario IS the dream scenario. And we CAN make it a reality for you, as we have for other men and women who have served.

For assistance with all strategic considerations regarding moving up to a larger home, let SoCalVAHomes help. Call us at 888-556-2018.

Chapter 8: Buyer Beware of a "Fixer"

The pros and cons of using Your VA Home Loan Benefit

to buy a house that needs some work.

As active military or as a Veteran, you have an extraordinary benefit with your VA loan. However, be cautious and plan carefully if your goal or your chosen property could be considered a "fixer-upper." There are clear advantages and disadvantages when buying this type of home using your VA financing.

One thing we at SoCalVAHomes have learned in working with our military and Veteran community is that many military members and Veterans are "Do-it-Yourselfers." You are skilled, independent minded individuals who, in many cases, would rather do the work yourselves than pay someone else to improve your property. We caution you to be realistic in your expectations and your budgeting.

Ask yourself, how much work needs to be done? Can you realistically budget the cost of materials? Is there anything in the scope of the projects that you can't do (electrical, plumbing, etc.) that you need to hire out and  therefore add to the budget? The bottom line is if the property can pass the VA appraisal inspection and still get financing, you need to be acutely aware and concerned with how much time and money you'll have to devote to the property.

When you buy this fixer-upper, how much work will be

needed to bring the property up to an acceptable standard that will make you and your family happy? Do you have that sort of time? Do you have the financial resources? Are you willing to take the time away from your spouse and/or family (if you are married and/or have children) to perform extensive renovations? Be very realistic when considering all this because long, drawn-out home improvement projects are known to cause high levels of stress in marriages and all relationships under that roof!

You must be prepared for the financial commitments necessary to bring the scope of the renovations to their conclusion. Homeowners constantly underestimate these costs. Big projects require significant cash. What is the best way to spend your money to get the biggest bang for your buck? Do-it-yourself or "DIY" projects may appear to be the most frugal way to achieve your goals, but ultimately will the reality match up with your initial plans and expectations?

Budgeting for home improvement projects can be very difficult. In our experience, our clients are thrilled to take advantage of the 100% financing afforded by the VA loan. It's much less common for our clients to have a significant savings account available to budget for home improvements after the home has been purchased. Financing of some sort is often needed for the next step of fixing up the home. If this is the case, what are the options for our committed do-it-yourselfers?

Financing options often only include credit cards or some type of installment loan, including those that attach liens on the new home. These options are typically offered with high rates between 9.9% and 21.9%. That is really expensive money, especially if it takes a while to pay it off. The larger the scope of the DIY projects on your new fixer-upper, the more caution we suggest you exercise. If you are planning a new kitchen, new bathroom, flooring, etc., plan on delays and additional unexpected expenses.

Another piece of advice is to not depend on home equity lines or cash-out refinances prematurely. Sometimes our clients assume that when they buy a piece of property, they can then qualify for an equity line and can pull cash out of the property relatively quickly. The reality is that most home equity line financing is available only to those who have perfect credit and have lots of equity. Banks will typically lend up to a combined loan balance of (first mortgage + equity line) 80% of the value of the property on a revolving home equity line. It will typically take years before most people build up enough equity to qualify for a home equity line of credit to finance home improvements. The same is true for a cash-out refinance, although you can likely finance up to 100% of the value of the home with a new VA loan. Still, if your purchase financing was 100%, how long to do think it will take for the property to appreciate so you can take a significant amount of cash back out?

Is it a big renovation job? Are you willing and able to commit the time and resources to complete the job in a specified time frame? Some new home owners take years. You probably have a friend who, when you go over to their house, they're still chipping away at big projects over months and months...or even years. When you've got multiple projects going on throughout a house, the overall completion time frame tends to dramatically expand. The more you take on, the more difficult it becomes to finish the details of each project. The overall finish of the house can look piece-meal and lack continuity or a consistent feel to it.

You may want to consider hiring a professional contractor for your improvements after the purchase. Of course the costs would be more than if it were a DIY project, but the result would likely be a finely remodeled home. When making all these decisions, factor in your time, the costs and savings and the finance charges, if you are not paying cash. Lastly consider the impact of the emotional stress on a spouse or family member related to home improvement projects. It is said that the top two reasons for divorce are family financial issues and anxiety stemming from large home improvement projects.

The other consideration might be one you don't want to evaluate just yet. How will all this affect your resale value? You're considering buying a "fixer," or you've just bought your home, and you're planning your remodel strategies…why think about selling? Not everyone stays in a home forever. We've got a very active database of thousands of homeowners who have used their VA benefit. Especially since active military homeowners get new orders and frequent PCS (personal change of station,) we track VA clients who are selling properties all the time. Again, be realistic. If you perform the work instead of a professional, will you be compromising the re-sale value of your home?

There are many important aspects to consider when you're thinking about buying a fixer-upper home as a do-it-yourself project. You might want to consider our Dreamweaver Home Purchase Process™ as an alternative.

If you're unsure about all the aspects of buying a "fixer," let SoCalVAHomes help. Call us at 888-556-2018.

CHAPTER 9: The Truth About VA Construction Financing

VA Construction Loans and VA Renovation Loans

In our experience there are two types of clients who consider building a home using their VA Home Loan Benefit. The first

type of client typically desires more of a "rural" living experience – more land and more open space than that which is available from a typical Southern California "tract" home. We understand this desire...*perhaps to recreate an environment that feels more like home, maybe where you grew up in the Midwest.* If you fall into the second group, you may have started your home search and come to the conclusion that, "This is tough going - it's a competitive game trying to buy a home using my VA." Many VA buyers in various markets also arrive at this same conclusion. Some buyers are even driven to the thought that, "Hey, if I can't easily buy a home on the market, why don't I build my own? I'll show THEM that I can get a home! Maybe I can even get a custom home built in a peaceful location...ahhhh, this will be great!" Yes...we've heard this many times.

You're not alone. Many ambitious and frustrated VA buyers have walked down this path before you. We encourage your enthusiasm, so we're going to clearly describe the challenges you face as your pursue this goal. There are solutions, but approaching your task with eyes wide open will be necessary for survival and success. When trying to borrow this money to buy a piece of land and build a home, you'll be better prepared if you understand the lender's point of view. This is risky business.

To chase this dream of building your home, it's important to understand how the "VA Guaranty" on "VA Construction Financing" minimizes the risk for the lender. Let's first define the **VA Guaranty**. The VA Guaranty binds The United States Department of Veterans Affairs and a lender together for the purpose of reducing the lender's risk. Lenders are institutional, private enterprise, for-profit, non-government entities, typically a bank or mortgage company. Provided the loan package meets all the VA loan underwriting guidelines, the contract between the VA and the lender says that the VA will protect the first 25% of the loan balance against loss, should the borrower fail to repay the loan.

If the borrower defaults on the payments, the lender will foreclose on the house and may suffer a loss when the home is resold. If the risk was properly measured in underwriting, the loss will hopefully be less than 25% of the original loan balance when the home is resold. In this case, the lender will have not suffered any financial loss and the mechanism between the VA and the lender will have performed as planned. The VA Loan Guaranty is paid for from an "insurance pool" funded by the "VA Funding Fee." This is an insurance premium or fee that is added to the loan balance, and directly paid to the VA from the lender after funding. Because it is part of the loan balance, it is paid for over the life of the loan by the borrower.

Obviously the VA Home Loan Benefit has plenty of advantages, including no down payment, more forgiving credit guidelines, and competitive interest rates. However, despite the existence of such a program, there are few (if any) lenders who will take the multiple layers of risk involved to make a construction loan, with a VA Guaranty. If you are going to be successful in your quest to build a home using VA construction

financing, you'll need to clearly understand the lender's point of view – their RISKS.

Lenders making VA loans operate from self-interest. They are primarily motivated by earning profit. When deciding to make a loan or not, no "charitable thoughts" are part of the process. Again, VA loans are not provided directly from the government. And because lenders are not willing to undertake unreasonable risks, it is very difficult (but not impossible) to get VA construction financing or a VA construction loan. From their perspective, if they have to foreclose, what factors below will cause a loan loss to exceed the 25% VA Loan Guaranty?

Risks Associated with the Economy (During Construction)

This risk assessment by all conventional lenders and VA lenders alike definitely takes into account overall "macroeconomic" factors. How is the economy doing? Are home prices rising? Is employment improving? In a really good economy and a hot housing market, it may be more probable for a smaller mortgage company to stake out a niche in VA construction lending. It would be much less likely for a big commercial bank such as Wells Fargo, Bank of America, Chase or Citibank to attempt such an endeavor. It's too specialized of a lending area and "outside of the box" of conventional thinking.

Risks Associated With Financing or Owning Undeveloped Land

Consider the realities of launching a significant construction project such as building a house. An owner, or lender in this case, has to make the money available to buy a piece of land and hope that the land and eventually the newly built home doesn't depreciate in value during construction. Construction can take six to twelve months or more. The piece of real estate has ultimately achieved its optimal value only when the construction is complete. Because the VA borrower will typically want to finance 100% of that finished value, the lender takes 100% (less the 25% VA Guaranty) of the risk with the hope that the entire project gets completed according to plans. If it doesn't get completed as planned, the lender has to foreclose on a partially constructed home whose current value would be very difficult to determine – a lender's worst nightmare.

Risks Associated With the Quality and Integrity of the Appraised Value

With a construction loan, an appraiser needs to be hired up front, using both the appraised land value plus the architect's final plans, to give a total value of the home when completed. All of this is done UP FRONT before the construction gets started. You would think this might be an easy task. However, the appraiser has to use recent comparable sales of "like properties" in the "neighborhood" that the subject property is located in. The big problem exists when these construction projects are conceived in less populated areas. These are communities typically with little sales activity due to a more rural location. And in these locations, the housing "density" is sparse because of larger parcels of land.

In this situation properties are much further apart and they sell less frequently than in suburban areas. As a result, finding comparable sales that meet ideal, typical appraisal guidelines can be difficult. Without a high frequency of geographically concentrated recent comparable sales, the appraiser has insufficient data to arrive at a potential value of the completed home.

Risks Associated with the Blend of Land Value vs. the Newly Constructed Dwelling's Value

Concerns also exist regarding the land value vs. the "improvements." The improvements are all the dwellings and amenities built on or into the land. Too much land skews the relationship of land value vs. the dwelling value on the total appraisal value. It's very difficult for a lender to get comfortable with an appraisal that has those characteristics. As an example, a property with a 1000 square foot home built on a 20 acre parcel is not going to be easily financed. Whereas a 2500 square foot home built on less than five acres is going to have a better chance at getting a loan. Land-only prices and values tend to be more volatile over time. Recognizing this, lenders don't like homes with lots of acreage and small dwellings. They prefer the opposite - big dwellings and less land equal less risk.

In our market in Southern California, there is tremendous housing density. Yet, on a home just outside of densely populated areas such as in East San Diego County, appraisals can be difficult for these reasons mentioned. This is a point of frustration for VA borrowers who are abundant in San Diego. Many want to build in a more rural setting. Don't give up on your dreams, sometimes it can be done!

Risks Associated With the Contractor Responsible for Completion of Construction

A lender doing any volume in VA construction loans would have to create systems to manage a whole list of separate risks, including qualifying the contractor who will be hired for construction. In a typical conventional construction loan where a large down payment is required to either buy the land or obtain construction financing or both, tons of documentation is necessary from the contractor. Underwriters want resumes, referrals from previous projects, licenses, insurance, bonding, etc. There is a very serious vetting process that takes place as part of the construction loan underwriting process. Let's discuss the execution of the construction project. The contractor has to complete the house in the prescribed time frame (9-12 months) and in the manner in which the plans describe. Do you know anyone who has ever had a problem with a contractor? It's a given if you do enough construction and renovation business.

Risks Associated with the Borrower's Changing Qualifications

There are potential risks to consider regarding the borrower. Will the borrower maintain their credit and income qualifications over the 9-12 months that it takes to complete the project? What if the borrower loses their job and their income? Or what if a borrower has serious health issues and their finances and credit suffer? A lot can happen in people's lives during this time frame. What if the active military member or Veteran is barely qualified, having JUST enough income to qualify? And what if rates go up rapidly during the year that it takes to build the house and that disqualifies the borrower? We've witnessed rates rise by 1.50% in just five weeks! You typically don't lock in a rate in for a year, but you can at great expense. If a sudden big hiccup occurs in any way with the would-be homeowner, the borrower would not qualify for the financing.

Reducing Risks with Two Step Construction Loans

In conventional construction financing, there are typically two types of construction loans or processes. The first and much more common construction loan process is a two-step process. The first step is the construction financing. This loan is wholly and separately underwritten for its own merits based on lender profitability and its associated risks of loss. When the construction of the home is complete, the second step or "permanent financing" is applied for separately. It is underwritten, funded and closed in the same way all other conventional loans are performed. This two-step closing process breaks the risk associated with the entire project into two separate pieces.

The second type of conventional construction loan in the marketplace is a single step or "single-close" loan called a "construction-to-permanent" loan. As of the second edition of this book in 2016, one source, and only one source that we are aware of, is attempting to fund "VA construction-to-permanent" single-close loans. Much of the same risks outlined above need to be addressed by the lender to make a success of this channel of business. It's difficult, but it is possible.

All Risks Accounted for...How to Get What You Want Using Your VA Home Loan Benefit

Unfortunately, there is a lot of misleading information online regarding the subject of VA construction loans and VA construction financing. With the limited information from the U.S. Department of Veterans Affairs available on the va.gov site, you might be led to believe that these loans readily exist. When you

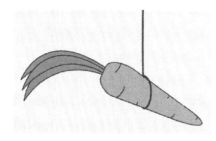

search for information online, it's not uncommon for lenders to "bait" you with advertisements, where they dangle a carrot of the possibility of a VA construction loan to get your attention. Once they have your attention and get your hopes up, they glaze over the reality or try to "switch" your attention to applying for a typical VA loan. I guess they hope you change your mind about your dreams of building a home, and you return to them to discuss a typical VA loan.

It is important that you get this information now, and that you know the challenges right from the start. Again, VA construction financing or a VA construction loan is a rare breed indeed. The reality is about reducing risk for the lender. It can be done under the right circumstances. So what does all this mean for you?

SoCalVAHomes was created especially to address the limitations of the VA loan. Our innovations have created possibilities for active military and Veteran home buyers that didn't previously exists. **Two possibilities exist for you in your quest to utilize your VA Home Loan Benefit to achieve a custom constructed home.** Utilize our single-close construction-to-permanent VA loan. Again, this will mean that all the right circumstances exist to minimize the lender's risk.

Your second option is to take advantage of our SoCalVAHomes Dreamweaver Home Purchase Process™. With this process, you tell us where you want to live and the ideal elements and amenities you want your home to have. SoCalVAHomes can then purchase the lot and build the home you want with our cash. You can literally build your dream house for zero down and zero closing. When the construction is fully completed, the home is transferred (sold) to you by using your VA financing to conclude the purchase. It's a TALL order, and it may sound too good to be true, but if you view the video testimonials on our website, you'll see the results we've delivered for our clients.

Chapter 10: Financing that Facilitates the "Fixer Upper"

Buying to renovate: The FHA 203k, a VA Financing Alternative?

You have a VA benefit and want to use it to create an ideal home, one way or another. There are many flavors of the VA loan, and your job (or a lender's job) is to find a match between your eligibility and the right mortgage. Although VA loans are usually easier than other loans to qualify for, sometimes you can't get everything you want with a VA loan. Home owner hopefuls often get creative and seek out other loans they have heard about, usually with mixed results.

In the spirit of exploring loan options, let's compare and contrast another government loan, the FHA 203K renovation Loan, with VA financing alternatives. The FHA 203K has been around "forever," and has both advantages and disadvantages. The FHA 203K is a housing rehabilitation loan, sponsored by the Federal Housing Administration, a division of HUD – The Department of U.S. Housing and Urban Development. This FHA loan program was created so that lenders would have a product for buyers who want to purchase and repair a fixer-upper as a path to home ownership.

Advantages of this type of mortgage include somewhat easy eligibility criteria. Another perk of this loan is that it covers both the property costs and home repair costs, as well as a 10-20% contingency for expenses beyond initial rehab estimates. And it is 100% guaranteed or insured by the federal government.

But there are disadvantages as well. The biggest one is that you are required to live on the property during the construction.

Don't make the mistake of being too easygoing with that idea, thinking that you'll sacrifice anything to be in your own home.

Living in a house that is being built/remodeled is a nightmare, especially if you've just bought it! Being in a house that has even a small remodel (such as a bathroom or the kitchen) is horrible, so few can imagine living in a house where the entire place is being rebuilt. That can strain your nerves, your pocketbook, and your relationships. Not the best of new beginnings. Unfortunately finances and home remodels are among the top reasons for divorce, so proceed with caution!

Further disadvantages include the fact that FHA 203K loans take longer to close than other products (60 to 90 days as opposed to the more common 30 to 45 days), and in the lending world, an extra two month wait in an ever-changing financial landscape can sometimes be the difference between making and breaking purchase deals. In addition to a high down payment, these loans have a "relatively" higher interest rate. Also, because it is a specialty loan, it requires a lender with specialized knowledge, which makes securing this rehab loan complex and less certain.

Still, the key to success is for you to do your homework and learn about the various loans that are available to you. To that end, compare and contrast the FHA 203k with a product that is very popular among active military and Veterans, the VA loan, especially in regard to mortgage insurance. A snapshot of the math makes things clear. Let's say that you are buying a house for the price of $100,000. Your final VA loan amount will be $100,000 + $2,150 = $102,150. The VA funding fee for the first time users of their entitlement is 2.15% of the "base" loan amount. There is no monthly mortgage insurance premium, as is the case with a FHA loan. In contrast, the FHA monthly mortgage insurance premium has risen and fallen based on the "financial health" of the program. The monthly premium has been as low as 0.50% and as high as

1.35%. At 1.35%, the premium for a $100,000 loan adds another $112.50/month. That's like increasing your interest rate from 5.00% to 6.35%!

The FHA loan has a higher "insurance premium" *because* the mortgage is 100% insured by the government, and the lender passes that risk of default and subsequent foreclosure expense onto the borrower. The VA Guaranty provides protection for only the first 25% of the loan balance to the lender. That difference can be huge to the lenders. And unlike the VA loan (where the underwriting requirements don't require any surplus in your bank account, the FHA loan typically requires a couple months of reserves (2x your total loan payment) to protect against a catastrophe such as losing your job. Additionally, the FHA loan requires at least a 3.5% down payment. Three and one half percent! Most VA buyers don't have 3.50% to put down. Thus the FHA loan is so expensive that most VA buyers don't want it or can't afford it. And, really, most buyers don't want to rehab a home themselves anyway. You may find that the FHA 203K works for you...but not everybody will. Perhaps a comparison chart will highlight the differences:

	FHA 203k Loan	VA Loan
Down Payment	3.50%	ZERO
Up Front Insurance added to the loan	1.75%	2.15% for the first time user
Monthly Insurance Premium	1.35%	ZERO

Cash reserves required	2 months	ZERO
Minimum credit scores	500-580	500-580
Ability to finance renovations	Yes	No

FHA sets guidelines for the types of properties and the nature of repairs that qualify for their program.

Property Types that Qualify for the 203k Loan

- Established homes that can be moved to a different foundation.
- FHA approved condos.
- Single-, two-, three-, or four-plex dwelling
- Existing homes under construction, yet unfinished (must be at least one-year old).
- Teardowns: a house where part of the building's foundation remains.

Repairs That Qualify for the 203k Loan

- Room additions.
- Second-story additions.
- Bathroom and kitchen remodels.
- Siding.
- Site grading.
- Completing a basement or attic.
- Disability access.
- Plumbing.

- Roofing.
- Flooring.
- Energy efficient home improvements.
- Repair, completion, and/or upgrade of patios and decks.
- Heating, air conditioning, and ventilation.

If you're interested in purchasing a home that needs renovation, is there another alternative? Yes. SoCalVAHomes specializes in understanding the entire spectrum of VA home buyers, including those buyers wanting something different and unique. The SoCalVAHomes Dreamweaver Home Purchase Process™ is a revolutionary concept. With this process, SoCalVAHomes offers a fully custom renovated home to an active military or Veteran home buyer for zero down payment and no closing costs. Ideally utilizing the Dreamweaver Home Purchase Process™, you get the right home for you, where you want it, the way you want it, with nothing out of pocket.

For assistance with purchasing and renovating a home, let SoCalVAHomes help. Call us at 888-556-2018.

Chapter 11: Factory Direct Homes!

Modular and Manufactured Homes for VA Buyers

Manufactured homes are often called mobile homes, and they can be referred to with regard to their size as a "single-wide" or "double-wide." You've probably seen one on a huge flat bed truck being transported on the freeway. The double-wide would take two trucks, because it's twice as big! To obtain a real estate loan to purchase a manufactured home, they have to be affixed to a permanent foundation, not in a mobile home park on a rented space. Mobile home parks commonly make a business of renting the ground or space that the unit is parked on. This differentiation is the biggest distinction between a "mobile home" and a manufactured home. You can't get real estate financing on land that is leased or rented with a dwelling that can be towed away!

Double-wide manufactured homes can be a very economical living space, and when placed on a permanent foundation, on a piece land that you own, well that's "real property," the true definition of real estate! And this kind of home can get VA financing under certain circumstances.

Modular homes (or prefabricated homes) are very nice homes that modular home builders construct with a variety of floor plans. The dwelling is built out of several different stock parts, and the modular home company assembles  the prefabricated elements together on the lot very quickly. Modular homes are never assembled on a rental space. They are always constructed on a lot with a fixed or poured concrete foundation. The modular home could easily be considered an upgrade from the manufactured home. It is typically a larger home than the square footage available with a double-wide, and it usually has a more custom, roomy feel.

Still, the process of creating either finished home is a daunting task. Here's a sample checklist. You must:

- Qualify for the financing.
- Find a lot (with utilities or set up utilities).
- Find the right manufactured home or modular home builder.
- Ship the home to the site or assemble the house on the selected lot.
- Appraise the home and fund the purchase loan.
- Move in!

VA buyers, who are often raised in communities with lower costs for housing, are attracted to manufactured and modular homes because it seems very economical. Their logic is sound because someone may be able to purchase a lot for under $100,000. An attractive manufactured house may sell for as little as $50,000. The $150,000 price tag on the finished home (likely in a more rural area) may look very appealing compared to the cost of a $300,000 "tract" home in busy Southern California suburbia.

Your manufactured home *could* potentially cost much less than the Southern California tract home that was built 15-40 years ago. And it may be brand new! However, there are likely some drawbacks and difficult challenges to overcome if this is your plan. One obvious drawback or comparison could be the quality of construction and materials used to build the home. There is no comparable substitute for a typical "stick built" piece of real estate. "Stick built" is an industry term that describes the construction with "sticks" or two-by-four pieces of wood, common with nearly all typical real estate.

Let's assume you are agreeable to the quality associated with a manufactured or modular home. Let's also assume you want maximum VA financing at 100% of the finished value of the home. Your biggest hurdle will likely be for the appraiser to find accurate comparable sales.

If your subject property will be in an area that does not have several manufactured or modular homes that have recently been sold, it presents a problem. It is difficult for the lender to truly determine what the finished home will be worth, because the values of these alternatively constructed homes are typically lower than the values of the stick built homes. Without several, very recent comparable (manufactured or modular home) sales close to the subject property, the appraised value is then in question. In certain regions, these types of homes are simply not that popular. All loan underwriting, including VA underwriting, looks for the following information in a appraisal to get comfortable with the value stated from the appraiser:

- Comparable sales need to be of the same "asset class," same kind of construction.
- Recent comparable sales need to have closed within 6 months of appraisal date.
- Comparable sales need to be within close proximity, less than a mile away from the subject property.
- Comparable sales are to be of similar age, condition and amenities, if possible.

Manufactured homes tend to cluster together in the same communities, so sometimes this type of construction can work better for the buyer. Modular homes are a bit more of a rare breed, so the appraisals can be quite difficult. Without an appraisal that has solid comparable sales data, your loan won't get approved and your VA financing won't fund.

Of course, if you had the means, you could pay cash for both the lot and the home! Why worry about an appraisal and financing if you don't have to! Well, the tremendous benefits of VA financing enable you to get zero down and zero closing. Are there financing alternatives when trying to buy one of these types of homes? Yes. Some of these manufacturers will create their own financing at 11.9% - 15.9%, and they may require some sort of down payment. That can be an alternative to traditional real estate lending, but at credit card rates. Do you want to pay rates typical of "unsecured" lending (loans without liens recorded at the county) on real property? Why bother? You would be buying an inexpensive home with very expensive financing. Unfortunately, that is all too common though.

Some buyers may even pay cash for a lot. And then they finance the manufactured home with a 20% down payment at higher rates in the "teens!" The home manufacturer doesn't care about the foundation or if it's ultimately defined as real property. That financing is not like a real estate loan. That's more like an installment contract or a car loan because it's such a high rate. Some manufactured home companies provide that kind of financing because it's *hugely profitable*! They are not real estate lenders making "secured loans" (with recorded liens in the county office) on the land and the dwelling at lower rates.

By now, you know that *it's all about the financing.* If there are 100 lenders in the community that will make a VA loan, perhaps only 10% of them will underwrite and finance a manufactured or modular home. And the rate will always be 3/8$^{\%}$ to 1/2 % higher. The riskier deal is also going to come at a higher rate, because this type of real estate is considered less desirable. If the lender has to foreclose and re-sell the home, the universe of potential buyers who want a manufactured home will be smaller than normal. More risk = higher rates.

If you have managed to overcome the hurdles so far, you would still need to qualify for VA financing in the same manner that you would if you were buying a traditional home or even a custom renovated home through our Dreamweaver Home Purchase Process™. Remember, all loans are underwritten while considering equity, credit and income. Equity or the amount of down payment is not a consideration with VA financing. However, credit must meet minimum standards, and income must be able to support the new housing payment.

The idea of buying a manufactured home is sound. But to be successful in your purchase, you typically have to be in a community where this kind of transaction is common…not the exception. This plan can work for some people in some parts of the country. But most Southern California communities are not really ideal for this kind of transaction. The idea of living in a manufactured home tends to be more appealing in rural communities. Yet in rural communities the population density is such that the homes don't sell frequently enough to generate the proper selection of comparable sales to satisfy the appraisal, which as a result satisfies the lender. It can be done…but know what you are up against!

For assistance with purchasing a manufactured home, let SoCalVAHomes help. Call us at 888-556-2018.

Chapter 12: Surviving Spouse Benefits

How a surviving spouse can use the VA Home Loan Benefit

...and other surviving spouse benefits.

The United States Department of Veteran Affairs offers a variety of benefits to spouses, children, and parents of a service member who has died in active duty, or from an illness or injury  sustained during active duty. The following is an overview on surviving spouse and dependent benefits.

VA Home Loans

The VA helps eligible surviving spouses finance the purchase of homes and to refinance their current homes, through the VA home loan guaranty benefit. The VA Loan Guaranty helps protect lenders from loss if the borrower is unable to repay the loan. The VA home loan benefit can be used to purchase or build a new home, purchase a condo, repair and improve a current home, refinance an existing loan, purchase a manufactured home, and install energy efficient systems such as solar, heating or cooling systems.

Current law now includes surviving spouses in the eligibility guidelines for a VA home loan, and the Veteran did not need to die in a service-related manner for the spouse to be eligible. This change in the law now includes a surviving spouse of a Veteran who was totally disabled and who was eligible for compensation prior to death, for any cause. In general, VA home loan eligibility for surviving spouses now includes the following:

- If the Veteran died in service or from a service-related disability.
- If the Veteran was a prisoner of war (POW) or missing in action (MIA) for at least 90 days.
- If the Veteran was rated "continuously and totally" disabled and was eligible to receive disability compensation at the time of death. Or if the Veteran was disabled for ten years prior to death, or five years from date of discharge.
- If the surviving spouse has not remarried.

For surviving spouses, eligibility is based upon a good credit rating, sufficient income, a valid COE   and required occupancy. Home loans are provided through private lenders and mortgage companies, but the VA guarantees a portion of the loan allowing the lender to extend more favorable terms in the process. The surviving spouse can expect the following benefits from a VA home loan:

- No VA funding fee.
- As little as zero down on purchase loans up to $417,000 (more in some areas).
- Up to 100% refinancing of assessed value.
- No monthly mortgage insurance premiums.
- Low interest rates.
- No penalty for early pay off or balance reduction.
- VA Streamline refinancing, even if ineligible for full VA home loan benefits.

Dependency and Indemnity Compensation

The Dependency and Indemnity Compensation (DIC) benefit is a tax free monetary benefit available monthly to the surviving spouse, children and parents of a service member who died in active duty or from an injury or illness sustained during active duty or during training for duty. Eligibility requirements must be met in order to receive DIC.

For the surviving spouse to be eligible, the couple should have been married and cohabitating together for at least one year or had a child together. A surviving spouse may also be eligible for DIC if the Veteran died in a way that was not related to his or her service, but had been receiving VA disability compensation for at least ten years preceding death. In addition, if the Veteran was receiving VA disability compensation for a minimum of five years after release from active duty, the surviving spouse may also be eligible for DIC. Finally, the surviving spouse must not currently be remarried; however, once reaching the age of fifty seven, they can remarry and continue to receive DIC.

The children of the deceased Veteran are also eligible to receive DIC as a monthly, surviving child benefit. The children must be unmarried. Those who are under the age of eighteen, and those between the ages of eighteen and twenty three and also attending school, are eligible for DIC. Children who were severely disabled under the age of eighteen, and who remain disabled as an adult, might also be entitled to survivor benefits under DIC.

Parents of the deceased Veteran may also be eligible for DIC if they were financially dependent on the service member. Biological, adoptive and foster parents are included in this category. The parents must also have an income below the minimum level established by law in order to receive monthly DIC.

Survivors Pension

The Survivors Pension is also known as the death pension. The Survivors Pension is a tax-free monetary benefit for the surviving spouse or surviving children of a deceased service member who served during a time of war. The surviving spouse must have an income below the level established by law and not be remarried. The surviving children must be unmarried. For the surviving spouse and the surviving children to receive the Survivors Pension, the deceased Veteran must have served at least 90 days of active service, with at least one day of war time service, and discharged under conditions other than dishonorable. After 1980, the deceased Veteran must have served at least twenty four months of active duty, with at least one day during a war time period, and discharged under conditions other than dishonorable. Children of the deceased Veteran can receive the Survivors Pension if they are under the age of eighteen, or between the ages of 18-23 if they are attending school. In addition, Children who were severely disabled under the age of eighteen, and who remain permanently disabled and incapable of self-support as an adult, are also eligible.

Dependents' Educational Assistance Program (DEA)

The Dependents' Educational Assistance (DEA) Program and the Marine Gunnery Sergeant John David Fry Scholarship are the two main GI Bill programs that offer educational assistance to survivors and dependents of Veterans.

DEA programs are available to surviving dependents of Veterans who died while on active duty or due to a service-related injury or illness. Surviving dependents of Veterans who are permanently disabled as a result of service-related injury or illness are also eligible. DEA programs provide education assistance and training opportunities paid directly to the student in the form of a monthly monetary benefit. The Fry Scholarship provides post 9-11 benefits to the children and surviving spouses of service members who died during active duty after September 10, 2001. The Fry Scholarship provides tuition and fee payments paid directly to the school that the dependent or surviving spouse is attending. Dependents may be eligible for more than one of these programs, but in most cases, will need to choose between the DEA program or the Fry Scholarship during the application process. The chart below compares the DEA program and the Fry Scholarship.

Benefit	DEA	Fry Scholarship
Payment	$1021 paid monthly directly to the student	Full in-state tuition at a public institution. Up to $21,085 at a private institution. Books and supplies stipend up to $1000 paid directly to student for each term. Monthly housing allowance paid directly to student.
Duration	For surviving spouses, benefit can be used up to 20 years following death of service member.	For surviving dependents, up to 15 years following death of service member.
Maximum	45 months	36 months

# of months benefit can be used		
DIC concurrent eligibility	Yes	yes
Programs covered	• College, Business, Technical, or Vocational Programs • Certification Tests • Apprenticeship/ On-the-Job Training • Tutorial Assistance • Work-study	• College, Business, Technical, or Vocational Programs • Certification Tests • Apprenticeship/On -the-Job Training • Vocational flight training • Tutorial Assistance • Work-study

CHAMPVA

The Civilian Health and Medical Program is a health care program administered by the Department of Veteran Affairs. With this program, the VA shares in the costs of health care services and supplies to eligible enrollees. CHAMPVA should not be confused with TriCare (formerly known as CHAMPUS) which is a managed health care program administered through the Department of Defense for active duty and retired service members and their spouses, families and survivors. To be eligible for CHAMPVA, you cannot be eligible for TriCare. CHAMPVA enrolls the spouse, surviving spouse who has not remarried, and children of a Veteran who is permanently and totally disabled or who has died from a service related disability.

In general, CHAMPVA benefits include most health care services that are medically and psychologically necessary. Prescription benefits are cost-free via Meds by Mail or with a 25% cost-share via OptumRx, a retail pharmacy network available nationwide.

Burial Benefits

Burial benefits are available for spouses, surviving spouses, and children of Veterans, even if they predecease the Veteran. Benefits include burial in a national cemetery with the Veteran, perpetual care of the gravesite, and inscription on the Veteran's headstone, all at no cost to the family. Another way the VA helps with the financial strain and need to honor military members is by providing various burial benefits to families of service members and Veterans.

For assistance in using the VA home loan benefit as a surviving spouse, let SoCalVAHomes help. Call us at 888-556-2018.

Chapter 13: You're Entitled to Free Money - VA Housing Grants

Combining a Housing Grant with the SoCalVAHomes

Dreamweaver Home Purchase Process™

In this chapter we will discuss some very special VA housing grants that are offered by the Department of Veteran's Affairs, especially the Specially Adapted Housing Grant that can provide significant assistance to disabled Veterans when purchasing or renovating a home, using your VA benefits.

Disability has always been a part of my life. My brother had a stroke when he was twenty one, and he's nearly sixty now. Although he is independent in some ways, he needs a variety of support systems to live a full life. Also, I have a son who was diagnosed with autism when he was two. Now nineteen, he needs an even more rigorous set of support systems than my brother. And to live a full, satisfying life as an adult, my son's array of support systems must continue to evolve. So, my family just slightly exceeds the national average on prevalence of disability in our nation, which is about twenty percent, based on a statistic from the U.S. Census Bureau. According to the American Community Survey, almost 1.1 million Veterans ages eighteen and over reported having a service-connected disability rating of seventy percent or more. There is a measurable population of non-Veterans and Veterans alike with disabilities who need significant support systems.

Another statistic relevant to disability is the increased survival rate for soldiers who are wounded in battle. Due to improved body armor and improved emergency medical treatment techniques, warriors are coming home in ever increasing frequency and numbers, some with serious disabilities to contend with. As is the case with dramatically increasing numbers in autism, society has a responsibility to support those in our community with special needs. With the Specially Adapted Housing Grant, returning soldiers with special needs can be financially accommodated using their VA benefits. Additionally, SoCalVAHomes.org can combine the Specially Adapted Housing Grant with our Dreamweaver Home Purchase Process. This combination of resources can produce a very powerful impact when purchasing and renovating a home. The result can be a highly customized residence with features that maximize accommodations for disabilities and enhance the quality of life and enjoyment of the home for the Veteran.

Specially Adapted Housing Grant

This grant is primarily used when building, remodeling or purchasing a home to make it wheel-chair accessible, and to modify the home and reconstruct it any way to meet adaptive needs. And it's a big grant. It has increased continually over the years, and in 2015 is currently funding $70,465. In order to qualify for the grant, the Veteran must have a disability that falls into one of these categories: a complete loss of the use of extremities, blindness, or severe burns. Over the years, the specifics of the qualifying disabilities for these grants have slightly changed. If you (for whatever reason) don't qualify now, you'll certainly want to check back on the qualifications for this program in the future.

Special Housing Adaptation Grant

Although it has a similar name, a lesser grant is the Special Housing Adaptation Grant. This particular grant is intended to finance modifications to the home, so the Veteran can be more mobile in the household. With it, the homeowner can widen doorways and hallways, install wheel-chair access, etc. The grant is currently an amount of $14,093. Disability categories that are eligible for this grant include blindness in both eyes with a visual acuity of 2200 or less, loss of the use of both hands, or a severe burn injury.

Residential Assistance Grant

This grant is for those who need to modify a home when they intend to be living in their family member's home The VA is currently offering $30,934 as the maximum amount available to adapt a family member's home for the purpose of increasing the Veteran's mobility within that home. If that were to be combined with the Specialty Housing Adaptation Grant, the total grant increases to $53,020. That's a really significant benefit considering these funds are intended for transitional purposes. Certainly the goal would be to increase self-sufficiency and move from transitional housing with a family member to a personal residence.

Home Improvement and Structural Alterations Grant

The opportunity exists to combine some of these above grants with the Home Improvement and Structural Alterations Grant that funds as much as $6,800. This grant is for the continuation of treatment for the disability. Combined with the SAH grant, a Veteran can receive another $6,800. Combined with the SHA grant, a Veteran can receive another $2,000.

A Powerful Combination of Resources and Benefits

At SoCalVAHomes, we get excited about the opportunity to assist a Veteran who qualifies for a VA housing grant. In combination with our Dream Weaver Home Purchase Process, these VA grants can significantly enhance the finish of the residence for the Veteran. We're the only company that facilitates housing for Veterans (and active military) by providing a fully custom, renovated home using VA financing. We'll search the marketplace and find a home that you desire, buy that home for cash and renovate it in the manner that you want. Imagine adding $70,465 in grant funds to the final finished home. The results could be extraordinary.

New custom renovations such as a state-of-the-art kitchen, modified bathrooms, hardwood flooring, etc. can be combined with the all necessary additional modifications that are necessary to support your lifestyle. Combining the financial resources of our Dreamweaver Home Purchase Process™ with the Specially Adapted Housing Grant gives us, and you, a tremendous amount of "horsepower" to do some amazing things for you.

Financially speaking, you should be able to qualify for significant, traditional VA loan financing, and then combine the grant(s) on top of the VA loan benefit. This will create a large budget for the purchase and modification of the home. With our Dreamweaver Home Purchase Process™, the VA loan will typically finance the purchase and all the modifications and improvements. The VA appraisal must demonstrate the value of all the improvements in the total new value of the home. However, in this case, because the granted funds do not have to be repaid, we have the maximum flexibility and ability to apply these funds toward modifications WITHOUT any consideration as to their effect on the actual value or resale value of the home from the VA appraiser's stand point. We can do things to the home that would never be possible without combining these two programs. That is what is meant by a large budget! This is a VERY POWERFUL marriage of resources and benefits.

Let's discuss the economics of the qualifying for the VA loan. In general, the Veterans who qualify for these grants are getting tax-free disability payments. It is possible to receive service-connected disability or VA disability compensation and Social Security disability insurance (SSDI) at the same time. When we underwrite the final VA loan financing, we perform what we call a "grossing-up" of the tax-free income payments. In this scenario a VA loan underwriter effectively equates your income to the same income as a working individual, as if taxes were getting deducted from a paycheck. As an example, if you make $3,000 a month in disability income, it can be equated to making $3,750 a month in an underwriting scenario. And if you combine that figure with spousal income or other retirement income, you may qualify for a significant sum of VA loan financing. Your credit profile and other debts will also be considered. Your disability payments are permanent, so you should be able to properly budget your income and expenses to afford truly special results when building out a new custom home.

For guidance in applying for these grants, simply give our office a call. Ultimately, you'll need to discuss your qualifications, complete VA Form 26-4555 and submit the application to the VA Regional Benefit Office nearest you. The VA Regional Benefit Office will not help you with the VA loan financing because the VA doesn't do loans - they only provide the "VA Guaranty" to institutional lenders who make the VA loans. SoCalVAHomes provides the VA financing. The VA Regional Benefit Office will only process and approve the grant. During the process of grant approval, we can initiate plans to move forward on your home ownership goals. You can apply for the grant online as well. If you're not familiar with ebenefits.va.gov, getting familiar with that site can be very helpful. You can obtain your Certificate of Eligibility there, or call us at 1-888-556-2018 and we can help you with these details.

Chapter 14: Gold Mine or Coal Mine? The CalVet Loan

Advantages and Disadvantages of a CalVet loan

vs. a Traditional VA Home Loan

People often call SoCalVAHomes inquiring about the CalVet loan, wondering if it might be a good fit for them. Our answer is it CAL🐻VET might be (if they are active military or a Veteran and a California resident). Like any loan, there are both advantages and disadvantages. In a few isolated circumstances, a CalVet loan may be preferable to a traditional VA Home Loan. In this chapter, we will compare and contrast their features and benefits.

Loan Limits

A big advantage of the CalVet loan may be the loan limit, depending on the amount of your financing needs. In 2015, CalVet loans had a loan limit of $521,250. That's significantly higher than the VA conforming loan limit of $417,000 throughout the state. California has a lot of "high-cost" communities where the county loan limit has been much higher than $417,000. A few years ago, in Alameda, Marin, and other select counties, the Department of Veterans Affairs, not CalVet, was actually approving 100% financing in these counties up to a million dollars.

In the counties where high-cost loan limits don't exist, CalVet financing may be an advantage to the extent that your purchase needs 100% financing.

If you are purchasing a home in a county that does not have a high cost limit (the loan limit is $417,000), and you want to buy a more expensive property, a "small" down payment will be required for a traditional VA home loan. The VA is going to ask that you cover that 25% guaranty or contribute 25% of the difference between the purchase price and the VA loan limit, which is $417,000 in counties without the high cost designation. If the difference is small, you may want to find a way to come up with the extra cash and choose a traditional VA home loan. But if you just absolutely have to have 100% financing, then CalVet might be an option for you because of that higher loan limit of $521,250.

Credit Standards

The CalVet loan is also advantageous because it is more lenient on those borrowers who have had credit troubles. In CalVet's case, all of the underwriting is done "old-school," via manual underwriting. Manual underwriting is when a human (not a computer) initially reviews your loan application. With CalVet, underwriters are instructed to be more flexible when considering derogatory credit.

However, manual underwriting can also work to your advantage with a traditional VA underwriter. Traditional VA financing with manual underwriting may accept credit scores as low as 580 or even lower, but the lender will adjust the "price" of the loan (the interest rate and points) to accordingly reflect the greater default risk associated with the lower scores. Considering CalVet has one "price" to fit all borrowers, it's my opinion, that CalVet is more of a last resort option when considering credit. CalVet rates and fees are a comparative disadvantage.

If you have had bankruptcies, foreclosures and/or lots of collection accounts and charge-offs, but you are now financially stable, CalVet's manual underwriting strategy may suit your needs. CalVet is not "credit-score-driven," per se, and that can be an advantage. For those borrowers who are at the very lowest end of the credit spectrum, CalVet may be your only option. Our advice is to explore all traditional VA financing options first before inquiring about a CalVet loan.

Mobile Homes

If you wish to buy a mobile home, CalVet will perform financing on mobile homes when you intend to rent the space to place the home on. These spaces are commonly in mobile home parks. These are not considered real estate loans. These are consumer loans because there is no "real property." In this case, you can load the home on a trailer and drive it away. That's not considered "real estate," or real property. In the typical world of real estate lending, that type of consumer financing doesn't exist because the mobile home is not on a fixed foundation; it's not attached to the earth! If you are looking for that type of residential living, CalVet presents an obvious advantage. In 2015, CalVet required a down payment. A 6-1/2% down payment would allow purchase prices up to $175,000. That's a lot of buying power for a mobile home purchase.

Rates/Loan Pricing – the Most Critical Comparison

In 2015, CalVet's charged a 1% origination fee, without exception. That fee on 1.00% of the loan balance needs to be paid to CalVet before closing. Therefore, an immediate price comparison would reveal the price of the CalVet loan as appearing to be more expensive. That's the only fee they charge. In typical VA financing, that 1% origination fee can easily disappear. Understanding "loan pricing," and how that 1.00% disappears is very valuable. There is a big difference in the mechanics of the moving parts of where CalVet gets its money to lend vs. where the funds come from when a traditional VA lender makes a loan to you.

With CalVet, the money to lend is created from selling "California bonds" to investors before you apply for a loan. The investors are promised a specific yield or rate of return on their investment based on current market conditions. When those funds raised from investors are exhausted, the program sells a new block of bonds in the same manner, likely at a different rate as market forces dictate. CalVet has more than one program. Let's imagine there is one hundred million dollars available to lend for one CalVet program and a hundred million dollars for another CalVet program. The interest rates on these mortgage programs go up and down as funds are loaned to borrowers and then new rounds of bonds are sold to investors. And in most interest rate environments, the CalVet rates are going to be *higher* than typical VA rates.

The CalVet system and "cycle" of raising funds, then lending those funds appears archaic as compared to the "real time" functioning of traditional mortgage banking. The system that traditional lenders use when selling VA loans "to the secondary market" or "GNMA" is far more efficient and responsive to the daily change in interest rates. This traditional system typically creates lower rates with expanded choices for different interest rates. And those choices can create advantages when addressing your closing costs.

CalVet's inability to absorb closing costs

In 2015, it was a "seller's" market. Due to The Great Recession of 2011, California had the lowest inventory of homes available for sale in the Golden State in fifteen years. In the years 2011-2013, all the first-time buyers came out of the woodwork at the same time. The renewed buyer demand and investors both helped to bid up prices. The result was that there weren't many homes for sale! It was a very tight market. And in tight markets, sellers are not inclined to give buyers any concessions for closing costs. The attitude is, "Here's the property as is. Buy it at this full list price or higher or get out of the way of the next ten offers! We're not giving away any credit towards closing costs or repairs or anything else!"

Here's when it gets really, really difficult with CalVet. If CalVet is the only option that will work for you, then be prepared to pay your own closing costs. When constructing what's described in the industry as a "VA no-no", a no-money-down-no-closing-costs purchase, the closing costs do exist and have to be paid somehow. And in that "VA no-no" scenario, closing costs will be paid for by one of two parties: the seller or the lender. In a tight market, the seller is NOT going to pay for them, and these costs can be substantial.

If you don't have any money and the seller is not going to pay for the closing costs, who's going to pay the 1% origination fee charged by CalVet? Who's going to pay for the appraisal, title, and escrow fees? Who's going to contribute the funds to the new "impound account," to budget for taxes and insurance? Someone's got to pay for all this! The seller's not going to pay for it, you don't have any money, and CalVet won't pay for it, so you are out of luck. With traditional VA financing, interest rate choices should exist to solve this problem. It's very common for VA borrowers to consider a higher interest rate option (than the lowest rates offered) where the lender pays for all of the closing costs. These options are a function of a complex capital market for mortgages.

In 1977, Lewis Ranieri of Solomon Brothers created the advent of "mortgage-backed securities." As a result, today there is a spectrum of interest rates available in the mortgage marketplace. The lowest rates, where you pay "points," are very costly. With the highest rate choices, the lender contributes funds available for closing costs. For an expanded discussion of how this works, please refer to the chapter on VA IRRRLs.

Imagine interest rates offered in a range between 3.25% and 4.25%. That interest rate spectrum allows you choices. At the highest rate of 4.25%, the lender can inject cash into the transaction to pay for all the closing costs including underwriting, title, appraisal, escrow, funding the new impound account, (months of property tax liabilities and home owner's insurance.) This can be very advantageous because closing costs can easily add up to more than $10,000.00. This is the mechanism of how costs typically get paid for in a VA purchase transaction.

Of course the opposite choice is also always available. Think of this choice as "buying points" or a "buy-down" as it commonly referred to. You (or the seller) contribute funds to buy down the rate in this case to 3.25%. Hopefully, whoever you're talking with to arrange your financing presents you with these valuable options. You do have choices.

In conclusion, from the loan "pricing" perspective or the availability of interest rate choices, Cal Vet represents a big disadvantage, whereas traditional VA financing offers choices which represent a huge advantage.

For assistance in determining which financing option is best for you, let SoCalVAHomes help. Call us at 888-556-2018.

Chapter 15: A Terrific Tax Exemption for Disabled Veterans

How Do You Qualify for and Reduce or Eliminate

Your Real Estate Property Taxes?

When you are awarded a service connected disability status from the Department of Veterans Affairs, there are typically TWO significant financial benefits to using your VA Home Loan Benefit. You are exempt from the VA funding fee, and that exemption reduces your home loan financing costs. (See other  chapters for more information on the VA funding fee.) You may also qualify for a significant reduction, or complete elimination of your property tax payments. As a Veteran, these benefits present an even greater reason to purchase a home.

However, the property tax exemptions are "state specific." Each state in the union has its own tax code dictating whether you, as a disabled Veteran, can claim any exemption from the property tax assessment, delivered by the county in which you own your home. Real estate property taxes are assessed by the county tax assessor, not the state. In California, where SoCalVAHomes operates, Article XIII of the California Constitution, Section 4(a) and Revenue and Taxation Code, Section 205.5 provides for this available exemption.

As an example of state to state differences, Texas allows a 100% exemption from all property taxes for 100% service connected disabled Veterans, regardless of your property value.

California is not as generous. The Golden State sets larger restrictions on property value, income and disability status.

Texas will allow reduced exemptions for those Veterans with LESS THAN 100% disability. California will only allow an exemption for Veterans with a full 100% disability rating. You must be a "qualified" disabled Veteran or the unmarried spouse of a "qualified disabled Veteran" to participate in the program.

In 2015, California allowed an exemption for the first $126,380 of property value. In other words, if you own a home worth $426,380 as assessed by the county assessor, your county will require that you still pay property taxes on $426,380 minus $120,380 or $300,000 of value. The Golden State gets a little bit more generous if your income is less than $56,751 per year. It's worth noting that California does not make any further restrictions if any of the income is tax free (from your disability payments from the VA.) If you meet that income criteria of less than $56,751, your property tax exemption increases to $189,571. California's tax code provides for annual inflation adjusted limits of both exemption amounts and income limits.

We see a lot of Veterans in the Golden State purchase property in less populated areas where prices are low. Areas which are more rural are much less expensive, and attract those buyers that yearn for a lifestyle better suited for less populated areas. Many of the Veterans who purchase homes in these areas meet the income restriction. For these men and women who have this specific income level, a 100% service connected disability, and the increased tax exemption, their economic benefit can be really significant. With property taxes slightly more than 1.00% of the value of the average home in California, this tax exemption is worth more than $157/month (and rising) to these deserved Veterans.

Applying for these tax exemptions can be relatively simple. Each county requires submission of a two page form (which has two pages of instructions) along with proof of disability. Your disability award letter will provide the necessary proof. The forms are available at the county tax assessor's office or easily downloaded online.

It's worth noting that outdated information appears on the California State Board of Equalization website. The information does not include over a decade of inflation adjustments on both exemption limits and income limits. Rather, current limits can be found at the bottom of the actual submission forms from each county.

Finally, although property tax payments are tax deductible, and may reduce your federal and state income tax liability, and although your disability payments are non-taxable, when you buy a home, you still must pay property taxes in many cases. The Disabled Veteran's Property Tax Exemption can be a very helpful way to enhance your affordability of a home in California. Be sure to consult your CPA regarding tax advice.

For assistance on determining what an affordable home loan payment could be for you, especially considering tax exemptions related to your service connected disability, let SoCalVAHomes help. Call us at 888-556-2018.

Chapter 16: Why You Shouldn't Cry Over Credit

Your credit score is NOT as important as you may think when buying a home using your VA Home Loan Benefit!

Are you concerned about your credit score and if it may disqualify you from getting VA financing for your home purchase? If so, you are not alone.

SoCalVAHomes.org, the innovator of VA home ownership processes and programs, does not want you to worry about your credit score! Surprisingly, your credit score may not be nearly as important as you might think, especially as it relates to VA financing. Many people are uncomfortable with the idea of a credit score. It sometimes feels like the adult version of being graded in school. For some, a credit score is like an invisible force hovering out there somewhere just waiting to judge you and destroy your dreams.

But credit scores are merely a way for lending institutions to try and predict future behavior. Credit scores are an attempt to create, via statistics, a magic crystal ball of sorts to gauge your ability to repay a loan.

Your credit report contains lots of information including:

- Credit risk scores, typically from Fair Isaac Co. – "FICO" scores.
- The consistency of how you pay your bills.
- Which bills you've missed or paid late.
- The types of credit that you applied for (inquiries regarding mortgage loans, auto loans, consumer financing, installment payments, revolving credit).

- Your payment history on each type of loan including the capacity or limit of a particular piece of revolving credit, as well as how much outstanding balance you have relative to that limit.
- Any current debt amount you may hold.
- Who you are paying.
- When the account was opened.
- Whether it is still open.
- Whether you have any delinquencies.
- Whether the delinquencies are 30 days late, 60 days late, or 90 days late.
- When the late payments occurred.
- Whether you've gone into foreclosure on a particular mortgage.
- Whether the account is current now.
- Whether it's joint with you and your spouse.
- If it is an individual account.
- Any judgments or levies filed against you.
- Bankruptcies.

This very personal information is gathered by the major credit bureaus and then sold in formatted packages—primarily a credit report—to companies who (hopefully) want to extend you credit (such as an auto lender, mortgage company or a credit card company.) In short, your credit score seems to include most all of your personal information except your shoe size.

The Credit Risk Score was developed by Fair Isaac and Company (FICO) to assist financial companies in assessing risk. It may or may not bother some people to learn that Fair Isaac and Company is a private, for-profit company, not a governmental oversight department. There are two government agencies who provide oversight for credit bureaus: the Federal Trade Commission (FTC) and the COC (Comptroller of the Currency). Still, it may be jarring for some to know your personal data, your score, is purchased by a company in order to make a decision whether or not to issue you credit. Typically, lenders subscribe to the three main **national credit bureaus**, which are:

Equifax (1-800-685-1111)

Experian (1-888-397-3742)

TransUnion (1-800-680-7289)

Everything that is reported gets aggregated by the bureaus to produce your score(s). We assume at this point that some readers have gone sheet-white over the fact that your personal details are given the "Big Brother" treatment. You might also have paled from sheer stress, wondering what "number" you are given by the software analytic powers that be. STOP WORRYING!

As stated before, active military and Veterans have a specific advantage: VA financing criteria is really, really liberal in terms of the "credit quality" that VA underwriters will accept. The reason for their liberal credit underwriting guidelines is because the VA underwriters and their lenders have the backstop of the VA Guaranty—insuring up to 25% of the loan balance, backed by the U.S. government. This allows underwriters to accommodate credit scores that conventional guidelines would often deem too low. FICO scores range from 300 to 850, and conventional loan underwriting prefers credit risk scores of 700 or better. Yet, with the VA Guaranty of 25% of the loan balance - the government-

backed insurance pool – much lower scores, as low as 500 might be considered. The bottom line is, if you have marginal credit…in the "fair to poor range," **YOU CAN LIKELY STILL BUY A HOME!**

Given this VA advantage, you can reconsider your credit risk scores. Is it really important to have high scores? In terms of qualifying for VA financing, the answer is No.

If you have previously determined to hold off from trying to buy a house because you thought your credit needs to improve, then you simply haven't properly evaluated your situation. There is hope!

That doesn't mean your **credit report** (a document that shows your credit history and scores) can be a disaster (e.g., you can't have a credit history filled with charge-offs, delinquencies and collection accounts and expect to be approved for a loan.) You need to work to keep your financial house in order. But if you had, for example, a bankruptcy or a life event such as an illness, and you resurrected yourself from all your crises and saved your credit profile, you are likely still able to get a loan or credit extended to you.

Let's explain this concept with some numbers. (We'll keep the Wall Street gibberish to a minimum.) Say a person with a credit risk score of 600 is offered a rate that would be approximately $3/16^{th}$ higher than a borrower who had "superior credit" or a 740 score. Well, $3/16^{th}$ isn't even ¼ of 1%. (It's just slightly higher than $1/8^{th}$.) And someone who had credit risk scores between 620 and 660 might be offered a rate that is $1/8^{th}$ of 1% higher than someone who had superior credit risk scores of 720 or higher.

Both of these lower credit risk score profiles are getting offered pretty good rates, all things considered.

Such is the difference between loan offers for lower credit scores, with the involvement of the VA Guaranty. Got a credit risk score of 600? That's not a great score but you can still get a good loan, thanks to your service and the VA Guaranty. The VA Guaranty, facilitated by the "VA Funding Fee," the money that goes into the "Guaranty pool" is the huge benefit that makes the whole thing work.

The reason we are telling you about the importance (or lack thereof) of credit score is to give the you, the VA buyer, a more complete picture of what you are up against…and where you can catch a break. People may be discouraged by their credit score and think that they need to improve it before they can pursue homeownership. If you are holding off trying to buy a house because you think your credit needs to improve, you may be shooting yourself in the foot! VA financing is likely already available to you with competitive rates. Those thoughts that your credit needs to be better are more applicable to conventional underwriting on conventional loans.

Here is where the VA Guaranty comes in, which is your green light to pursue a loan and ultimately own a home, regardless of your credit score. Let's say you decide to wait for the perfect moment when you have improved your credit score to a traditionally good score of 700+. Okay, but what if during that time of improving your credit, interest rates rise 1% and prices go up 10%? Your ability to afford a property is dramatically affected, and the payment for the same house is now approximately 23% higher. The chance to purchase that house may just have slipped through your fingers. Big mistake!

The VA Guaranty is the lender's "risk adjustor" that allows

them to take a risk on you. Statistically, VA loans default at a rate much higher that of their conventional loan counterparts. The VA Guaranty of 25% dramatically reduces the lender's risk of loss, in the same manner that a 20%-25% down payment reduces the risk for the conventional lender. Essentially, the VA Guaranty absorbs the risk that is comparable to the typical down payment. Advantage Veteran! Don't make your credit blemishes an excuse to defer considering purchasing a home. Again, that would be a mistake.

Hopefully you now understand why we CAN make the statement, "Credit scores are NOT that important!" They have only a marginal effect on the rates available to VA loan applicants. Because the VA program is the lending marketplace's credit risk equalizer, it eliminates the necessity of superior credit that is required for conventional financing.

Finally, don't rely on credit risk scores that are generated anywhere other than an application for a mortgage loan. These credit risk scores are derived from the FICO score "software versions" necessary for a mortgage application. The credit reports will generally produce two to three credit risk scores. **Consumer credit monitoring systems use different FICO software versions, typically producing a single score.** Again, this score can be dramatically different than those scores obtained by mortgage lenders. Relying on your credit monitoring system's single "consumer version score" can be very misleading when it comes time to apply for a mortgage. *There can be a big difference in the single consumer score vs. the "middle score" of the three scores produced by a credit report for a mortgage application.* This could potentially create a false sense of security for you if you are only using these "other scores" as your credit monitoring measurements.

For assistance in discovering your scores and viewing your entire credit report, let SoCalVAHomes help. Call us at 888-556-2018.

Chapter 17: Misleading Credit Monitoring Systems

Why You Shouldn't Trust Credit Monitoring Systems.

If you are concerned about the safety and protection of your credit report and credit accounts, you might have considered signing up for a credit monitoring service. However, for most people credit monitoring is misleading when it comes to measuring your credit risk scores in preparation for a home purchase using your VA Home Loan Benefit.

Of course, the idea behind credit monitoring is a good one, as simple and obvious as saying, "Lock your front door." Safety can go a long way. You always want and need your credit report and  credit cards to be free from errors and fraud. Credit monitoring services may work for some people who want peace of mind, but you really don't need to pay a specialty service to track your credit scores and inform you of unusual activity. These days, banks and credit card companies aggressively monitor for fraud protection and many offer credit monitoring services for free as a value-added service. This is good, but it falls short when preparing to apply for a mortgage.

The way to best protect your credit is to educate yourself about credit basics, and then monitor your credit on your own. How well do you understand your credit score and credit report? Many people have heard about credit scores from the colorful commercials that have been on the airwaves. Many of these "free services" get your attention and then present an up-sell to sell you paid services. Often folks don't think about their own credit health until they need to open a new credit card or obtain a loan. Your credit score doesn't automatically give someone an a green light to loan a certain dollar amount, but rather it is a gauge that suggests your credit worthiness to lenders. It represents your likelihood and ability to repay a loan. Lenders are assessing the risk of default when they are loaning you money.

Most Americans have at least heard the term "FICO score," though many dismiss it if they aren't looking to open a credit card or negotiate an installment loan. Who wants to know their creditworthiness until they absolutely must? FICO, or Fair Isaac Co., is a company that created the FICO score, a number arrived at by utilizing information provided by the three major national credit reporting bureaus: Equifax, Experian, and Trans Union. As it relates to applying for a mortgage loan, a credit agency (kind of like a broker of credit data) will give a mortgage lender the ability to check your credit from each of the three bureaus. This data is extracted from the three bureaus simultaneously and commonly filtered through three different versions of the FICO scoring model, resulting in the production of your credit risk scores. It is common for Experian to use FICO V.2.0, Trans Union to use FICO Classic.4.0, and Equifax to use BEACON 5.0 FICO. These scores often differ depending on the different credit bureau. Some creditors don't even report to the top national bureaus. **When differing data, collected by each bureau, is pumped though different software versions, this produces different scores on your report!**

A key point for you to understand is that a credit monitoring system is likely monitoring only one bureau and likely NOT utilizing the same FICO software versions that the mortgage industry uses. When it comes to applying for the largest piece of credit in your life, your home loan, your credit monitoring system may literally have you blindfolded, as your "mortgage credit scores" might appear much different than what you had been monitoring and hoping for.

Let's look at the value a credit monitoring service brings to the table. A credit monitoring service monitors your credit report and sends you a text, email or letter should any unusual activity occur. While you want to monitor your credit to have the best error-free credit score possible, a credit monitoring service often monitors your information at only one of three credit bureaus, while you hope that your number and information is similar across the board. Buying an incomplete credit report is as helpful as purchasing a bucket with a hole in it.

Worse, credit monitoring services are sometimes claiming to sell you something they can't actually deliver - protection. While there are bona fide identity-theft protection products such as LifeLock, a credit monitoring service is less valuable as identity theft protection despite their claims.

Identity theft is a nightmare because criminals who obtain personal information find a way to open credit cards and banks accounts and even obtain loans based on your name and credit. Credit monitoring services are simply not equipped to handle such surveillance. An all-encompassing identity theft protection company, unlike a credit monitoring service, networks with hundreds of companies—from auto lenders, to retail, to pay day institutions, to black market websites. And, because the network is directly affiliated with the identity theft protection company, you can be notified of suspicious activity…often in minutes.

By contrast, if suspicious activity occurs in one of your accounts or on your credit card, a credit monitoring service likely does not have the network that an identity theft company may have. The reporting of any suspicious activity must first go to a credit bureau—a middle man of sorts—who will contact you much later. Also, a credit card company or bank doesn't have the insurance that a company like Life Lock has, nor the resources to spend up to one million dollars hiring experts to track your case and expedite your credit recovery efforts. An identity theft protection company can shield your credit in ways that credit monitoring services simply can not. (We do not specifically endorse any particular identity theft company.)

Why spend $120 to $240 a year on a credit monitoring service that provides such minimal value? In fact, credit monitoring services can be dangerously misleading. It's like someone reassuring you that they set your burglar alarm when they did not. That creates a false confidence that could come back to haunt you.

Would it be better to do it yourself! There are a few common sense things that you can to do, and we will provide a guideline. You might even find monitoring your own credit kind of fun. It certainly is interesting! Taking personal responsibility for your money and credit is the foundation and beginning of wealth creation. Managing your finances well means creating opportunity and options. Here are some proactive things you can do:

- Ask your bank and each of your credit card companies if they report to all three credit bureaus.
- Be on the alert for companies who promise too much. A credit monitoring service, as stated above, cannot prevent identity theft. The most they can do is alert you about unusual activity on your accounts, and then only after the fact.
- If you do receive warnings from your bank or credit institutions, heed them! Pay attention! Address the issue! Consider yourself warned and take further steps to protect your credit and your name.
- Don't fall for the credit monitoring services that claim they are free. They likely are not. The only free credit reporting

is through the bureaus themselves. They all offer a free credit report once a year. Get it every year.

- Purchase your "tri-merge" credit report from a mortgage lender. Even purchasing it four times a year is less expensive and more accurate than using a credit monitoring service.
- Review each transaction of every bank and credit card account.
- Always work with banking and credit institutions you trust.
- Develop a personal relationship with those in your bank.
- Protect yourself in a myriad of ways. Don't carry your social security card with you, and be leery of giving out your social security number.
- Keep your financial information and income tax files in a secure place.
- Shred sensitive documents, anything that has information about you.
- Raise your privacy setting, which are tools on the internet and social media. Privacy settings control who can see your data (and most importantly, who can't).
- Limit personal information on your social media sites. It is foolish to list your birthday, pet and/or children's names, mother's maiden name, etc. That information is the very substance of security questions used by banking institutions to prove your identity!
- If you believe or fear a card has been compromised, cancel it for security and peace of mind.
- Monitor your bank statements relentlessly for fraudulent charges.
- Be careful where you use your debit card, including using ATMs in bad neighborhoods or where a machine is not in plain sight. Ambitious thieves use what are called "skimming machines" to steal information off your card.

- Verify who is asking for information or passwords and on whose behalf and why.
- Be extra careful at restaurants or bars or anyplace where your credit card is taken out of sight.
- Protect your information from computer malware. Identity thieves can use malware to infect your computer and steal information. To counter, always run your security updates. Learn how malware works, and in order to counter it, turn on your firewall and limit those who have access to your computer.
- Use a Credit Security Freeze (also known as a **credit freeze**, a **security freeze**, or **credit report freeze**.) A credit freeze prevents others from seeing your credit report and prevents new credit from being issued if someone other than you applies for a new account, credit card, or a loan in your name. A credit freeze is certainly an inconvenience for you, but it is a tool in your arsenal. It offers you a defensive strategy unlike any other protective measure.
- Ask one of the three credit bureaus to put a fraud alert on your credit report. According to the Federal Trade Commission, they must tell the other two companies. An initial fraud alert can make it harder for an identity thief to open more accounts in your name. The alert lasts ninety days but you can renew it.

To obtain a copy of your mortgage credit report, let SoCalVAHomes help. Call us at 888-556-2018.

Chapter 18: When You Need a Down Payment

Should You Borrow from Your Retirement Plan or Liquidate Your Retirement Plan? Down Payment Options When Borrowing More Than the County VA Loan Limit

Current "conforming VA loan limits" allow for 100% financing on a home purchase up to $417,000, including the VA funding fee. Thanks to the Housing and Economic Recovery Act of 2008, "high cost" loan limits are now established at the beginning of each year for counties where real estate prices are more costly. These higher loan amounts provide for 100% financing, for loan amounts in excess of $417,000.

But what if you want to finance a home purchase in excess of the county loan limit? VA loan amount guidelines will require that you contribute a down payment equal to 25% of the funds between the loan limit and the purchase price. Effectively, you provide the 25% "VA Guaranty" on the loan in excess of the loan limit, in the same way the VA guarantees 25% of the entire loan balance against default for the lender.

This brings up the question, *if you want to buy a home, and you need a down payment, where are you going to pull the money from?* If you were responsible enough to start saving for retirement at an early age, don't sabotage your plan by liquidating those funds just because you think you need the cash for a down payment...or any other reason for that matter. **Leave your retirement funds alone!**

There are as many reasons for needing money as there are people who need it. When tough times fall upon folks and emergencies come up, people looking for funds too often consider looting their own retirement account. You can practically hear their thought process: *"I've got this retirement account, and right now I need money. I'm young and could solve my problem by cashing out this account now and someday replace these funds."*

People in this position will often overlook actually borrowing the money as a solution, a smart financial strategy. Borrowing money, especially from a retirement plan, is a complicated subject. We live in a nation that gives mixed messages, saying both debt is wrong and at the same time, leverage (controlling an asset with borrowed money) can be good and can even build wealth. Leverage can also help you be a better steward of your own finances.

If you have established a retirement account, you are most likely able to borrow money from it. You MUST consider borrowing against it as an option to solve your cash crisis rather than liquidating the funds altogether.

Although there are plenty of reasons to borrow from your retirement, there are also several valid reasons NOT to borrow from your retirement account. My chapter on fundamental financial planning for Veterans and military families of suggests the need for an "emergency fund" to be established first, so these kinds of events don't force difficult financial decisions such as deciding to borrow from your retirement account.

Let's examine many of the advantages of borrowing retirement funds rather than liquidating retirement funds. Wouldn't you rather borrow money from *yourself* than close out and liquidate your most important fund representing your greatest long term financial security? While the idea may initially sound counter-intuitive, borrowing money can be a smart, strategic financial decision. In the context of borrowing for your down payment, if your proposed debt ratio (your proposed monthly debt payments divided by your gross income) will allow you to borrow a bit more, that plan of action will likely be far more productive for your financial well-being and your retirement strategy. You can typically borrow up to 50% of your retirement funds without penalty. The advantages include:

- Often a better rate of interest than unsecured consumer loans.

- Pay yourself back with interest.

- Avoiding penalties and income tax liabilities.

Again, I'm not distributing tax advice, but if you chose to liquidate, the amount withdrawn from your plan would now be subject to income taxes, the opposite of what you achieved when you deducted the contribution from your taxable income in the year you contributed. When you choose to liquidate the funds from your retirement, *income tax would be immediately withheld upon distribution.* You would need to consider that subtraction from your funds when budgeting for a down payment. Alternatively, when borrowing against your retirement fund as opposed to liquidating, you'll avoid the tax liability.

Additionally, there exists an early withdrawal penalty when liquidating your retirement plan before the age of 59 ½ However, there are a variety of exceptions to the 10% early withdrawal penalty, including military exceptions. Members of the military reserves also can receive early IRA distributions without being subject to the penalty under the following circumstances.

- You were ordered or called to active duty after Sept. 11, 2001.

- You were ordered or called to active duty for a period of more than 179 days or for an indefinite period because you are a member of a reserve unit.
- The distribution is from an IRA or from an elective-deferral plan, such as a 401(k) or 403(b) plan or a similar arrangement and taken during the active duty period.
- Early IRA withdrawals also are penalty-free in a few other instances, including a first time home purchase. Anyone, including Veterans can currently take advantage of this first-time homebuyer exemption. You qualify under this tax rule as long as you (or your spouse) didn't own a principal residence at any time during the previous two years. This wouldn't apply if you were selling your home and buying a larger home. And that's a common circumstance when our VA buyers need some extra money for the down payment on the new larger home.

The primary focus of this chapter was to contrast borrowing vs. liquidating. However, there a plenty of valid reasons NOT to borrow from your retirement account. The following are important points to consider:

- Payments for mortgage interest or payments on a business loan are tax deductible. Payments to your retirement plan are not tax deductible. Therefore, you're repaying your retirement loan with "after-tax money" (income that has already been taxed), and then later, when you withdraw the funds in retirement, you'll pay taxes on that same money again. In this manner, borrowing against your retirement plan could be considered paying taxes twice.

- In many plans, borrowing money from your 401(k) means that you're selling positions that are invested, equal to the loan amount. You'll be forgoing the potential profits and the power of compounding your returns when the investments appreciate. And as you pay back the loan, you're repurchasing the previously sold shares but at current (and probably higher) prices.

- Some plans won't allow you to contribute to your 401(k) until you've paid off your loan.

- Many retirement plan loans must be repaid within five years. If you can't repay in that time frame, your employer will treat the loan balance as a distribution, triggering income taxes and the ten percent early withdrawal penalty if you're under age 59½. You could also be denied the opportunity of contributing to the plan in the future.

- If you leave your job, the loan may become due and payable within a short period of time. If you don't repay the loan when due, the IRS will consider the unpaid balance to be taxable income.

The MOST important reason NOT to borrow OR to liquidate from your retirement account is what you are compromising! Ultimately you'll need to retire AND live somewhere, likely in a home that you own. I know it's hard to consider bothgoals of home ownership and retirement. But the time to allow your retirement investments to compound and the act of exercising consistency in your contributions are the key elements to success in retirement planning. It is important to save at every age, especially in the beginning of your career, so that your nest egg has time to grow. Don't make the mistake of thinking that you are too young to save for retirement. You only have so much time in this life to invest. And that time, allowing your investments to experience compounded growth, makes all the difference in the world! For a more detailed discussion, see the chapter, *Mission Control: Financial Success for Life.*

For assistance in determining what your appropriate down payment should be to meet your needs and the means by which to obtain your down payment, let SoCalVAHomes help. Call us at 888-556-2018.

Chapter 19: Paying "Extra" On Your Loan – Mortgage Rigor Mortis!

Beware.....This could be your biggest financial mistake!

This is likely the most important chapter in this book! We have consulted hundreds of Veterans who seem continually intent, in our opinion, on making the mistake of paying extra on their mortgage. A lot of clients call and tell us that they want to pay off their loan in order to be debt free. The advantage of paying off your mortgage is singular and clear. You have the security of owning your home outright and being debt free. Surely that is a long term goal to which everyone aspires to, right?

Though paying off your mortgage is an idea (even a value) that most people subscribe to, we don't believe in it and don't recommend it. There are a number of disadvantages, in our opinion, that outweigh any advantage when it comes to smart management of your finances. Frankly, this common and easy mistake to make, represents…**a very slow financial death.**

Accelerated Loss of Your Tax Deduction

As you pay down your mortgage, with every payment you make, you are reducing the principal. This is the built-in, mathematical concept know as loan "amortization." Each payment consists of principal and interest. Amortization pays down your mortgage balance in such a way that each loan payment on a 30 year loan is composed of mostly interest in the beginning years and nearly all principal in the final years. The combination of principal and interest within each payment slowly changes over time. With amortization in play, the next month's interest expense is lower than the previous month because the balance is paying down. Paying down your loan balance may sound like a good idea, but it reduces your annual interest expense, and this will affect your tax liability.

Most tax payers enjoy the deduction that the interest expense on their home loan offers when they "itemize" their deductions on their Schedule A of their federal tax returns. If you're already enjoying that deduction, and you are "paying extra" on your mortgage, you are accelerating or speeding up the LOSS of that important tax deduction. Normal amortization will naturally reduce this deduction over time as less interest expense is charged due to reducing principal balance. **But WHY would anyone want to potentially *increase the speed* of paying MORE in taxes each year?**

Your tax deduction essentially lowers your "net effective rate" on your mortgage. If you have a 30 year mortgage for 4.00% and your income puts you in a 25% tax bracket, your interest rate is *effectively* about 3.00% because of your tax deduction applied on your Schedule A. As an example, if your $100,000 mortgage is at a 4.00% rate, you would pay approximately $4000 in interest expense in the loan in the first year. If your tax bracket is 25%, you would pay approximately $20,000 in total income taxes on an income of $80,000. However, because mortgage interest is tax deductible, you would likely deduct that $4000 of interest expense from your gross income and pay taxes on only $76,000 in income. At the tax bracket of 25%, your tax liability is reduced to 0.25 X $76,000 or $19,000. Your mortgage interest deduction saved you $1,000 in income tax payments! You could easily argue that your "net effective interest rate" was actually 3.00% on your mortgage. Because your $100,000 loan at a rate of 3.00% would only cost approximately $3000 in interest expense in the first year. Therefore, having a rate of 4.00% with a tax deduction (in a 25% tax bracket) is like having a 3.00% rate without a tax deduction due to the $1000 difference. Since all primary mortgage interest expense from your owner occupied home can be deducted (consult your CPA), having a 4.00% interest rate is REALLY like paying at a rate of 3.00%. Your "net effective after-tax rate" is even lower than 3.00%, if you're in a higher tax bracket. (Again, consult your C.P.A. or tax professional.)

Perhaps the idea of never paying off your mortgage goes against the grain of your upbringing or your common sense. The historical roots of our society's motivation and determination to pay off our mortgages actually stems from the Great Depression. Massive foreclosures occurred when people lost their jobs and couldn't make their payments. The natural response in managing family finances in the aftermath was the initiative to be debt free. A similar occurrence developed in the years following the financial crisis of 2008. The reality of these lessons learned from shockwaves in our economy is a lesson in personal financial management. One of the simple concepts we discuss in this book is the establishment of an emergency fund. Yes, to survive the economy's "shock treatment" may take a large emergency fund for some, but that's the point.

Most of us are raised and taught to work hard, save money, and pay our bills. We agree, yet we're still opposed to the idea of accelerating your mortgage payments by paying extra on your loan. It may sound or feel uncomfortable at first as you attempt to get used to the idea of staying in debt for your own benefit. The majority of Americans have been taught that paying off debt is both morally correct and financially smart. Unfortunately, the majority of Americans retire broke with Social Security as their primary source of income – a sad, but true statistic.

Loss of Your Liquidity

When you are paying down a mortgage you are eliminating your liquidity. Liquidity means cash in the bank. Liquidity means you have cash in investments that you can "liquidate" and convert to cash immediately, including stocks and bonds. When you are in an "illiquid" financial state, it means that you don't have much cash, or you don't have the ability to convert assets to cash quickly. This "financial state" or status is a recipe for potential financial disaster! Having a large emergency fund is the beginning ingredient of being liquid or having liquidity.

Here's what it might look like to make the mistake of paying extra on your mortgage and not have an appropriate emergency fund. Imagine your mortgage payment is $1500/month, but you have an aggressive plan to pay it off by writing a check for $2000 every month. That's admirable, but there are probably hundreds of ways you could use that extra $500/month to strengthen your finances, especially enhancing your emergency fund. Many people are worried about paying off their mortgage but don't have an emergency fund! That makes no sense at all. When a financial crisis hits those without an emergency fund, credit card balances begin to skyrocket.

If an unexpected financial crisis is a result of health problems (which is very common,) and insurance doesn't cover all the doctor bills, the result is often medical collections. If the credit card payments can't be made, charge-offs from these accounts appear on your credit report. Subsequently, new credit applications will be denied. If the situation is not corrected, the only option may be bankruptcy.

The bottom line is people who are more liquid in their financial management survive financial hardship far more effectively. They resurface on the other side of a crisis in much better shape than those who are illiquid and don't have any savings.

Accelerating your mortgage payments by paying extra on your loan is INCREASING your illiquid status. It is also increasing your likelihood of falling into a crisis mode should an unexpected financial shockwave occur that requires liquidity beyond your means. If your only asset is your home equity, your only options in response to such an occurrence is to borrow from your home IF, and I do mean IF, a loan is available. Your last resort would be to sell your home. And the real estate market climate, when there are large economic shockwaves, is never favorable. In these types of markets such as in 2008, investors who are liquid are like opportunistic carnivores, feeding on the demise of other's misfortunes. In other words, investors make up a large portion of the universe of buyers in this type of market when there exists financial chaos. And investors only buy homes at discounted prices. If you're forced to sell in this kind of climate, you're not going to get the price you want.

When you are prepaying your mortgage, it means that you've stuck your money into your home…where it is…*stuck*. If you are paying down the mortgage, you are building equity, but you've converted a liquid asset into an asset that is very illiquid. Why would you want to take *your money* and use it to eliminate liquidity?

Let's look at it another way. You are paying off debt that is only costing you 3% - 4% a year, where as an investment advisor could give you a half dozen investment ideas where you might be able to make 4% - 10% annually. You may think you don't have enough money to have such an advisor, but you might be surprised to know that large investment companies, such as Vanguard, Fidelity, Oppenheimer, etc., will often accept contributions as low as $50/month to their investment funds. And as the founder of SoCalVAHomes, I consider myself qualified to offer investment ideas. I have more than thity years of investing experience and previously held Series 3, 6, and 63 securities licenses.

What is "Cheap Debt?"

Of course, the conservative thing to do would be to pay off your mortgage. In our opinion, that is not the *smartest* thing to do, especially when debt is so cheap right now. And debt will always be cheap, relatively speaking. What exactly is cheap debt, and why is it "relatively" cheap?

Cheap debt could be defined as an **"inexpensive interest rates" relative to the opportunity cost of money.** Opportunity cost is a term, mostly used in finance, to describe the "cost" of not doing something or not participating in an investment. When an event produces a result, but you're not participating in that event and achieving that result, it's "costing" you the value of that result, not to participate. In this case, we're comparing a "cheap" interest rate to the return on an investment. For example, if your mortgage rate is 4% and the stock market goes up 15% in a year, the true opportunity cost of your money is the difference between the 4% your loan costs and the 15% earnings you can make by investing in the stock market. This example doesn't even consider the combined effect when including the tax deduction likely available from the mortgage interest expense.

In the above example, your opportunity cost of money is pretty high because the opportunity to participate in the stock market gains was a good opportunity! But again, why is debt always relatively "cheap"?

Debt or mortgages almost always have lower rates of interest than the opportunity cost, (yield or investment return,) of slightly riskier investments. As an investment strategy, you could actually invest in mortgages, taking the other side of the transaction as an investor, not a borrower. Money for mortgage loans comes from institutional and private investors. The relationship of rates as a borrower (with great credit) to returns on investments for stocks and other alternatives is almost always a relationship of lower borrowing rates to higher investment yields. Therefore, this debt is almost always "relatively cheap!"

In the years since the financial crisis of 2008, this relationship has demonstrated extraordinary opportunity costs. Debt was cheaper than ever because interest rates were held extremely low by the Federal Reserve's activities. To stimulate economic recovery, they lowered lending rates to banks (a common activity,) and through additional financial engineering known as "quantitative easing" (an unprecedented activity in the U.S.), they manufactured extremely low rates for an extended duration. Mortgage interest rates declined from approximately 6.00% to nearly 3.00%. In the heat of the financial crisis, stocks were badly beaten down, and in retrospect, the rebound in the stock market was sensational. If you had bought tons of stocks in 2009 (like Warren Buffett did) *you would have made a fortune in the following six years.*

Why are most people in a hurry to pay off such "cheap" debt when the opportunity cost of their money is so high? Take that money, and instead of disproportionately paying down debt or paying more on your mortgage, invest it elsewhere. Managing investments is something that everyone struggles with. It is natural to wonder where to put your money in every economic environment. But the bottom line is, your money needs to work hard for you.

Average returns in the stock market since the 1920s have been around 8%. In the recent years, the Dow Jones has traveled from its pre-crisis high in 2007 of about 14,200 down to about 6500, then back to about 18,000 in 2015. Stock market returns have been HUGE. Yet interest rates have been extremely low (and are often given credit for the much of the stock market gains). Super "cheap debt" was at 3% and 4%. So when debt is so cheap, don't pay it off. Stay in debt and put your extra funds into something that returns 8% such as stocks, or perhaps a conservative mutual fund that is a mix of stocks and bonds. Or maybe you could choose a *really* conservative mutual fund that invests in real estate such as a real estate investment trust. These are some *opportunities* which define the *opportunity cost* of money that makes debt *relatively cheap.*

The Realities of Retirement Can Be Negatively Affected By Paying Extra on Your Mortgage

This common financial strategy is about so much more than lower interest rates and appropriate financial management. It's about avoiding something truly sobering and terrifying statistics show that up to 75% of Americans will retire "broke", as defined as needing to live solely off social security. And a recent study predicts that 95% of baby boomers will die broke, leaving nothing to their heirs! When we say "paying off your mortgage is strategically unwise," we are also asking "Do you want to be like 75% of Americas who retire broke? Or do you want to be smart, use a sound financial strategy, *invest,* and create a portfolio that enriches your life and secures your future?"

Another thing to consider is whether it's advantageous to have tax deductions in your later years. If you're content with a retirement income of only social security or disability payments, you probably aren't going to have a tax problem in your later years and tax deductions won't be as important. But trust us, you *want* a tax problem! While that initially sounds as backwards as embracing debt, "having a tax problem" means that you have enough income to incur the tax liability (unlike those who are broke). Your tax deductions will be very valuable to you! If you have children who you currently declare as dependents, you will eventually lose those tax deductions as they become independent adults.

To master your financial horoscope and retirement planning, we shall now present the SoCalVAHomes Golden Financial Rules. Other chapters, such as *Mission Control: Financial Success for Life,* cover these topics as well.

- Establish an Emergency Fund. Have three to six months of income stashed in a savings account in case of ill-health, job loss, or disaster. We understand that it seems like a lot, but it's an essential part of a fundamentally sound plan.

- Use time and consistency as your mantra for retirement savings. Substantial wealth can be accumulated over time with consistency in your investment habits. Start early and invest every month. It's not a matter of where you invest, it's that you make a habit—a *discipline*—of investing. You need to make a commitment to regular, monthly, investing. It's not difficult. We can show you how. *That's* how you win over time!

- Take advantage of the benefits of home ownership. There are many! (See the previous chapter, *The Rational Renter vs. The Bold Buyer* for more details.)

A Case Study

Let's look at a real life example of a client of ours whom we will call J.R. J decided she wanted to pay off her mortgage because "she didn't want the payment." Her deceased husband was a successful saver, and she received a substantial sum from life insurance proceeds upon his passing. J wrote a $200,000 check to pay off her mortgage. She has a net worth of less than one million dollars, but she took $200,000 of those funds to pay off her mortgage when her payment was only $1500/mo.

She had eighteen years left on a 30 year loan. She could have had a new 30 year loan and refinanced that payment down to about $600/month. She could have also reduced her interest rate to 1% less than her current rate. There was every reason for her to refinance:

- Actually INCREASE the tax deduction (due to new amortization)
- Maintain exceptional liquidity.
- Dramatically lower her payments
- Increase her portfolio through additional return on investment

But instead, she lost the tax deduction on her primary residence. She lost the additional liquidity. If she wants that liquidity back she has to sell the home *or take out a new mortgage.* And finally, her opportunity cost on the $200,000 was significant if she would have invested it instead. Thus, in her effort to be debt free, she lost key benefits that would help her create additional wealth. Her attempt at financial management turned out to be unsophisticated and foolish.

Final Thoughts and the Compelling Math to Investing as Opposed to Paying Extra

Your goal for retirement should be to keep earning from investments similar to what you earned during your highest wage earning years. Ideally, you want to keep the lifestyle that you have now. And the lifestyle that you have now, typically includes paying some sort of housing expense, whether it is rent or a mortgage.

We're not oblivious to those of you saying that you hate debt and want out of it completely. But let's apply some math to *becoming debt free the smart way!* If the thought of becoming debt free makes you feel more comfortable during your retirement years, and you believe it will give you maximum peace of mind, then apply this investment strategy to your goal! The concept being conveyed here is to not incrementally accelerate the payoff your mortgage, but keep investing instead, and then one day, pay off the entire remaining balance in one single payment with your investment returns. Your investment yields will have produced much more money to then pay off your mortgage in a lump sum. Why is that? Because debt is always relatively cheaper than the opportunity cost of the alternative uses of your funds.

That is why most people invest in stocks throughout their working life and then convert to something more conservative in their retirement years, moving from stocks to bonds. Stocks historically have yielded greater returns than bonds. Using that concept, the smart money would say "If I want to be debt free and retired when I'm sixty, and I am currently forty years old, and I have just obtained a 30 year mortgage, why don't I take my extra money and consistently invest it to create a lump sum to pay off my mortgage in twenty years." This concept would maintain tax advantages and increase liquidity. For the next twenty years, this person could create wealth by properly allocating an extra few hundred dollars each month (that would have been used to pay down my mortgage) and invest it with the goal to be debt free by the age of sixty.

Essentially, the smart alternative is to invest in a mutual fund or similar diversified investment vehicle (hopefully with a tax qualified status.) Allow that investment to compound returns and multiply that capital for twenty years. Ultimately, given historical market performance, you will accumulate far more money than just the amount of debt that you were hoping to get rid of by paying extra on your mortgage.

Here's a numerical example: (I'll represent the numbers using digits for emphasis!)

Again, if you are 40 years old today and want to retire debt free at age 60, consider this strategy. Instead of aggressively applying your extra cash to pay down your mortgage for 20 years between the ages of 40 and 60, invest your discretionary cash into a mutual fund, hopefully into a "tax qualified" account such as an IRA, so you don't pay any taxes on the returns as the money grows. See the difference in wealth creation in the following example:

Let's assume you just funded your 250K mortgage and your interest rate is 4.00%. Your monthly payment of principal and interest is $1,193.54. Again, your goal is to pay off your 30 year mortgage in 20 years. To accelerate your payoff on your 30 year loan and get it paid off in 20 years, you've got to make a payment that of $1,514.95. That's an additional $321.41.

To reach your goal of becoming debt free in 20 years, the common, conservative approach would be to apply an extra

$321.41 a month to the loan for 20 years. Instead, what if you take the $321.41 a month and invest it (say at an 8.00% return) for 240 payments, in a mutual fund, tax qualified in an IRA. Those funds would accumulate to $189,317. Guess what the actual remaining loan balance would be after 20 years on the 30 year loan, when making the minimum $1,193.54 payments? The balance would be $117,885. If you take the $189,318 that you accumulated in your investment and simply pay off the remaining loan balance of $117,885, you come out $71,433 ahead in more ways than one!

Again, the common approach would be to make that $1,514.95 payment to be debt free after 240 payments or 20 years and NOT have that remaining $117,885 balance. IF you apply the extra money towards your mortgage your mortgage tax deduction is reduced more rapidly and you have less liquidity! We suggest avoiding those pitfalls and INVEST the extra money, not pay down your loan.

So do you still want to be part of the "herd" and pay extra on your loan? Or do you want to achieve your goal in a smarter way and invest your money and have an extra $71,433 in the bank when you retire debt free at the age of sixty? It's simple math. That's simple *investing*. That's the truth!

You need to behave like a bank: **the Bank of Me**. Banks take in deposits for checking accounts and CDs at some small interest rate they offer you, say 1.00%, and they lend it back out to those who need loans at THREE TIMES THE RATE, say 3.00%! Essentially, the bank "borrows" money from you and makes money from your money. Their mechanism for investment yield is lending at higher rates. You can create a similar arrangement, and attain similar investment yields, when you choose to NOT pay off your mortgage quickly and invest the extra cash. You can invest in other financial strategies that historically yield higher returns than the cost of the rate paid to the bank. Again, I can't stress this point enough. What do you think the banks are doing with your money? They are investing in loans (or other strategies), using your money to make a profit. Be the bank! Don't pay them off faster than you're required to!

For suggestions on how and where to invest, especially in a tax qualified account, I suggest you contact companies such as Vanguard and Charles Schwab for assistance, but you can always call us at SoCalVAHomes for help. Call us at 888-556-2018.

Chapter 20: Bogus Bi-Weekly Payments on Your Mortgage

Are bi-weekly payments on your mortgage a big mistake?

VA borrowers often wonder about bi-weekly payments, a common strategy to accelerate your mortgage payoff. The idea is to make payments every two weeks, rather than once a month, which adds up to making an extra monthly payment each year.

If you've read the chapter, *Paying "Extra" on Your Loan – Mortgage Rigormortis!,* you already know that we are not fans of accelerating your mortgage payments and principal reduction. However, the bi-weekly payment concept and its drawbacks and benefits deserves attention.

Bi-weekly payments are commonly structured as half the amount of a regular required monthly payment. The borrower divides a mortgage payment exactly in half and then pays that half mortgage payment every two weeks. The borrower effectively makes TWENTY SIX bi-weekly payments, equaling THIRTEEN whole mortgage payments over the TWELVE month year. That is a typical mortgage acceleration: paying off your loan faster than the amortization required for a 30 year loan. Is this a good idea? Would you achieve the same end result by adding $1/12^{th}$ of a payment onto your normal payment every month? Yes, and you would maintain much more flexibility with your monthly budgeting.

"Bi-weekly payments" often refer to a financial product, typically involving a fee to have a third party company set-up a payment system. Bi-weekly payment products, while still in existence today, were sold more often in the 1980's and 1990's by financial services intermediaries. A financial intermediary is someone who is a middleman between a financial institution (such as a credit union, bank or mortgage company,) and a borrower. Intermediaries and the companies for whom they work would make presentations pitching bi-weekly payments as beneficial, claiming:

- They are a useful tool that will save you a tremendous amount of money.
- It is easier to budget because the payments are smaller.
- You will pay off your loan faster, 7.1 years earlier on a 30 year loan.
- You save tons of interest expense as you speedily pay down the principal.
- You increase equity because you are reducing the principal and thus own more of your house (equity equals the value of property minus the debt owned on that property.)

The Problem with Bi-weekly Payment Products Sold By These Companies

Typically, because of the way the lenders in the U.S. mortgage marketplace structure loans, you are not allowed to pay "partial" payments or split your normal payment in half, twice a month on your mortgage. That is not how the "note" functions on our domestic mortgage products. The note requires that you pay the entire payment, typically on the first of the month. You are of course allowed to pay additional amounts on your mortgage, and we'll cover some elements of that topic in this chapter.

Remember we said there can be intermediaries who set up this bi-weekly payment program? Those intermediaries—perhaps a mortgage company, perhaps a mortgage broker or even an insurance agent—may sell you a biweekly payment product to manage your payments for you. You might buy into this program because you wish to shorten the length of your mortgage term and save money. And the seller of this program demonstrates how it magically saves you over seven years of payments – wow! The payments would then be sent to an "Escrow Account" at a financial services company. That company waits until at least a full payment has accumulated in your escrow account, and then it forwards your full monthly payment onto its final destination on the first of the month. Isn't it odd then, that you will find yourself facing extra charges for this "service" of "letting" you pay down your loan double-quick? In this arrangement, you'll typically pay a biweekly mortgage conversion set-up fee, which costs between $200 - $500. Then you'll get dinged again with a transaction fee of $2.95 - $9.95 each time *your* money is drafted into an intermediary's escrow account. And there your money will sit until it is time for your mortgage lender to accept it. Absurd!

Our main point of this discussion is that if you are ever approached to pay off your mortgage faster via a bi-weekly payment program facilitated by an intermediary, run away! You can achieve the same result yourself, without all the fees, by simply dividing your required payment by twelve (12) and adding $1/12^{th}$ of a payment onto *each* of your monthly payments. The net effect is making thirteen monthly payments in a calendar year.

The Bi-Monthly Mortgage

A "bi-monthly" mortgage could also be called a semi-monthly or bi-monthly payment.

 This is like the unicorn of American mortgage financing. It's is so rare we're not even sure it exists in our highly developed mortgage system. More complicated mortgage products such as these may be available in Canada or elsewhere around the globe. This next concept is important though because of the distinction of *how* the principal reduction and mortgage acceleration functions.

With a bi-monthly mortgage, you divide your monthly payment in half and make a payment twice a month, one payment on the 1st and the other on the 15th. Over the course of the year, semi-monthly payments result in twenty four payments. As opposed to reducing principal just once a month, and getting charged for interest on that new lower balance on the next payment, a little magic happens! The bi-monthly payments reduce principal twice a month. Because of the principal reduction in the middle of the month, the borrower is then being charged less interest expense between the 15th and the end of the month. This lower interest expense shows up on the amortization schedules for this type of loan.

With a bi-monthly mortgage, the lender would be posting the principal reduction that much faster with twice as many payments during a twelve month calendar. In theory, that would save the borrower a ton of interest expense compared to a normal 30 year amortization requiring only twelve monthly payments per year. This loan product is a rare beast indeed. We've never seen it used in the U.S. Again, it may be available in other countries.

Banks and Mortgage Companies Still Love "In-house" Bi-Weekly Payments!

This above heading sounds counter-intuitive based on our previous discussions. However, large lenders love automatic, scheduled payments from you. They love to put you in a "pre-authorized checking draft." They want to drag your payments right out of your checking account and into theirs. It's easier for them. They want predictability of payments without having to communicate with you, or having to wait for your money. They don't want delinquencies, and the last thing they want is foreclosure! They absolutely love it when they can pluck money out your account! That's why, at the beginning of your new mortgage, lenders will reach out and entice you into a bi-weekly payment program. They want to present to you an "advantage" for having your payments plucked out of your account. This is the same sales pitch as the one coming from an intermediary, but with a different motivation.

The lenders also like the bi-weekly because they are conceivably making money on the "float." They have your extra money in their coffers while it waits to be applied to your monthly payment. They are doing the same thing that the old third party administrators were doing. They are drafting right out of your checking account:

> On the 1st.
> Again on the 14$^{th.}$
> Again on the 28$^{th.}$
> And applying the full payment on the 1st of the next month!

The key to the success of a bi-monthly payment schedule is all about crediting that principal at the beginning *AND during the middle of the month*, something that doesn't happen with any of the bi-weekly programs available at the banks and mortgage companies. Because the principal isn't getting credited at twice the frequency, you are not getting the benefits that would accrue, given the correct mathematics.

If you find that you are being charged a service fee just to pull your own money out of your checking account—to heck with that! That's robbery. Avoid bi-weekly products that charge you scads of money for something you could do yourself. If you're looking to pay more on your mortgage to get ahead, then take the money you would pay in service fees and apply them to your mortgage and accelerate it that way!

Some VA borrowers who favor bi-weekly schedules are those people who get paid every two weeks as opposed to twice a month on the 1st and the 15th. There is a subtle difference here being paid TWENTY SIX times a year vs. TWENTY FOUR times a year! In our experience, these folks get easily enticed into these programs and adopt a bi-weekly payment schedule because it seems to make budgeting more manageable. If you fall into this category, just be realistic of how this game works and why it exists.

For assistance on which type of payment plan works best for your mortgage payment, let SoCalVAHomes help. Call us at 888-556-2018.

Chapter 21: The Secret Advantage of VA Disability Income

Why receiving Disability Income is an Economic Advantage for VA Home Loan Borrowers Especially When Getting a VA Cash-Out Refinance Loan

Veterans who have disabilities as a result of their military service are eligible for special benefits including, but not limited  to, remarkable terms on cash-out refinances. If you are a Veteran who suffered physical or mental disabilities during or post military service, you can apply to the U.S. Department of Veterans Affairs and the VA will reward you some level of Disability Benefits from as little as a 10% rating, up to 100%. Of course VA disability payments are the benefit that no one wants to need, though many are grateful it is available for our wounded American heroes.

In short, receiving a disability grant gives you an advantage with regard to the VA loan funding fee. The VA funding fee is unlike any other loan fee. Technically, the VA funding fee is contributed into an "insurance pool." This pool creates a U.S. government-backed partial guarantee for the lender, against borrower default. One economic advantage of receiving disability benefits is that *you are entirely exempt from paying the VA funding fee.* (See the notes on the VA funding fee in Chapter 2: *How To Buy a Lovely Home.*)

Being exempt from paying the funding fee is a big deal. It is not only a big chunk of change that does not get added to your loan balance, but it is a policy that can provide other huge advantages.

Let's look at a specific example and run some exact numbers. The financial health of the VA Guaranty is the funding fee. For a first time user, on a purchase loan, the VA funding fee is 2.15% on a zero down payment loan. As an example, if you are borrowing $300,000 for a no down payment purchase loan, 2.15% or $6,450 is added to your loan balance for a total loan amount of $306,450. Yet if you are receiving disability benefits, you are exempt from the VA funding fee, a savings of $6,450! That is a distinct advantage! All of the people who are fortunate enough to not receive disability benefits are supplementing you. You are getting the same amazing VA Home Loan Benefit, even though you aren't paying the funding fee, all while you *are* getting a very reasonable sum of tax-free money paid to you monthly in your disability income.

The Economic Advantage of Receiving Disability on VA Cash-Out Refinances.

Let's say that you're receiving disability and are exempt from having to pay the VA funding fee. Let's also imagine that you bought a house and after several years the house appreciates 25%. At this point, you want to take cash out of the home. A cash-out loan is a loan where your property is appraised, based on established guidelines, and you are allowed to take a certain amount of money out by funding a new larger loan amount. When receiving VA disability income, again, you are exempt from the VA funding fee. The VA guidelines are such that they'll allow the lender to do a cash-out loan all the way to 100% of the value of the home!

If you are not exempt, and you are not receiving Disability

payments from the VA, then your funding fee is 3.3% of the loan amount. If you apply for a $300,000 loan, the $9,900 gets added to that "base loan amount" for a total loan amount of $309,900, including the funding fee which gets added on top of the loan.

But the Veteran who receives Disability payments doesn't have to pay that 3.3%, that additional loan balance requires higher payments which add up fast!

Another advantage to receiving disability benefits is how such a cost effective cash-out refinance can help you consolidate debt. For example, if your house was purchased for $300,000, imagine that it appreciates to $325,000. Meanwhile, as it appreciates, you accumulate $25,000.00 of credit card debt. Perhaps rates drop 1%, and you want to take advantage of lower rates and pay off those credit cards. The Veteran without a disability rating would make payments on a new loan balance of $325,000 plus a funding fee of 3.3% or $10,725 for a total loan amount of $335,725. Contrast that with the Veteran who has a disability rating. He or she doesn't have to add the $10,725 to the new loan balance and make higher payments. that ability to do a cash-out refinance without the 3.3% funding fee radically reduces their closing costs on the VA cash-out loan. It becomes a much more efficient and economical way to access your equity compared to your counterpart who is paying that funding fee of 3.3%.

There are so many financially advantageous ways to apply the "discounted closing costs" that results from the exemption from the VA funding fee. The ability to access every bit of your home equity through a VA cash-out refinance and apply this discount is an incredible benefit. It should be considered a "staple" element in your toolbox to maximize the effectiveness in your financial planning.

Take advantage of the economic advantage of no VA funding fee on your refinance or next purchase. Let SoCalVAHomes help. Call us at 888-556-2018.

Chapter 22: The Cash-Out VA Refinance vs. An Equity Line

The pros and cons of financing options to improve your home or consolidate your debts.

Let's say you have a set of home improvement goals, but you don't have the needed cash on hand, so you decide to borrow the money. Or perhaps you want cash out of your home to consolidate your debts, or for *any other reason*, but you're not sure what your best options are, and you're just not certain of how to go about it. Since you need to borrow the money, your first objective should be how to borrow it at the lowest cost. Let's jump right into some examples…

Let's say that you received a loan to purchase your home at a rate of 3.25% and you never refinanced. Perhaps you've built up some equity, and a new loan rate of 4.50% is currently available. Do you want to take cash out on a new loan and replace the entire loan balance of your old loan at the 3.25% rate with a new 4.50% rate? Well, the math on that is going to be pretty easy. Depending on how big your 3.25% loan balance is in relation to how much cash you want to get out and the resulting new loan balance, you'll do the math and arrive at a decision. The larger your cash out needs are, and the less appealing the alternative financing options to meet your needs appear, the more likely you are to replace the old, lower rate with a higher one. You may even want to factor in the tax deductions* if you want to go down that road, and ultimately you'll come up with an answer of whether you think a new VA cash-out refinance is a good idea or not. *Consult your tax professional.

Here's an example of a bad idea. You financed a home purchase for $350,000 and you had a 3.25% rate, and all you want is $20,000 to do some things around the house (e.g., a new patio, fix up the kitchen, etc.). Most people aren't going to replace a 3.25% rate on a $350,000 loan with a new loan at a rate of 4.50% just because they want an extra $20,000. That would be poor money management. You'd really be increasing your interest rate on all your debt for very little benefit. You would naturally examine other financing alternatives to meet your needs of borrowing the $20,000.

Let's look at a different example. Maybe you bought the home long ago and it's now worth 400,000. Right now your loan balance is $150,000 at a rate of 4.00%, and you have a really aggressive home improvement project where you need $250,000 and literally want to take the maximum out on your VA loan amount to the entire value of your home. In this example, you're not going to worry so much about replacing an old, lower interest rate of 4.00% with a new rate of 4.50%, because the difference in rate is minimal, and you're dramatically increasing the size of your outstanding debt. And your other alternatives to obtaining the new $250,000 may look less appealing than using your VA benefit.

Equity, credit, and income are elements that are evaluated in every mortgage loan underwriting decision, including VA loans, equity lines and other home improvement loans. Each element is defined by its own specific characteristics, such as how much equity you have (in your home) or how superior your credit is, or the amount of your income in relation to all of your prospective debt payments and other monthly expenses you may be obligated to. The combination of all of these elements together will dictate your product choices in this decision as they also dictate an underwriter's willingness to approve your loan application.

Equity is defined as the difference between the value of your home and your loan balance. The equity, current loan amount, and your current rate are going to dictate in nearly all cases, how you're going to make your decision – whether you want to use a VA home loan to optimize getting <u>all</u> your equity out or another avenue. The distinct advantage that VA financing offers, in most cases, is that lenders who make VA home loans will make new loans all the way to 100% of the appraised value of the home. Other conventional mortgage options have limitations, typically to 80% of the appraised value of the home.

As in the last example, the VA cash-out option to 100% of property value can be a distinct advantage which will influence your decision of which product to choose. Other alternatives such as home equity lines of credit may limit your loan amount and not meet your cash needs.

Credit can be a major factor in these decisions. This can be the case for ALL financing alternatives from mortgage loans to secured home improvement loans (especially solar contracts) to unsecured options such as credit cards. When you're borrowing money and pulling cash out from your home's equity, especially using a VA home loan, a VA loan underwriter will carefully evaluate your credit.

To achieve success with this new VA home loan request, you'll need to have acceptable credit. If your credit risk scores are below 600, your offers for a cash-out VA refinance are going to be almost non-existent. You have to obtain a mortgage credit report and discover what your credit profile looks like. Do you qualify for a VA cash-out loan? Is it an option? In some cases, unfortunately the answer is going to be a "no." Once you've determined that your credit will allow you to qualify, you can consider whether a cash-out VA loan is the most valuable option to meet your needs.

Your **income** will be reviewed as well. Does your income allow you to qualify? An underwriter will ask you for proof of your income (W2s, paystubs, etc.,) People go through life and do have changes in their circumstances, especially changes in income. In some cases, you might not qualify because your income isn't sufficient for the new loan amount request. If a VA cash-out refinance is to be one of your financing alternatives, those three fundamentals of equity, credit and income really have to be addressed first.

Your **disability rating** can be a big factor in arriving at your decision to choose a VA cash-out loan. Of course no one really wants to be in the position of receiving disability benefits, but if your disability rating is at least 10%, you have a tremendous advantage when using your VA benefit, as relates to the VA cash-out home loan. The current VA funding fee for a cash-out home loan is 3.3% of the loan amount, added on top of the base VA loan amount. But when you are receiving disability payments, you are exempt from that funding fee. That cost advantage is huge when considering a VA cash-out loan. Loans can be structured with or without closing costs, depending on the rate you choose, and you SHOULD be offered a choice. If any costs exist on your VA cash-out refinance home loan, they are going to be added to the loan balance. This includes the VA funding fee. If you are disability rated, then you are exempt from paying the VA funding fee. That means much more money is available for your cash out needs, compared to those borrowers who ARE paying the VA funding fee, added to their loan balance. Ultimately, the cost to access the amount of money that you need is going to be a big decision making factor.

Another financing alternative would be a home equity line of credit, or a revolving home equity line. This home loan product will have many of the same underwriting requirements when reviewing equity, credit and income as the VA cash-out home loan does. An advantage of the home equity line of credit (HELOC) is often its cost. Typically when obtaining a revolving home equity line of credit, the transaction is free of closing costs. A disadvantage can be that the credit score requirements can often be high, and substantial amounts of remaining equity can be required. Another disadvantage might be the adjustable rates that are offered. Let's examine…

Let's say you have lots of equity and you have a VA home loan for $300,000 and a property worth $400,000, and you only want another $20,000 for home improvements. To get a $20,000 equity loan would mean your total outstanding combined loan balances would be $300,000 plus $20,000 equaling $320,000 combined, and that would be 80% of the value of your home. If you have good credit and enough income, you're going to get that home equity line for free from most commercial banks and credit unions. That's always going to be the cheapest way to initially borrow from your home, if you can.

Often there are VA borrowers in our market who have built some equity. They've accumulated say…10% to 20% equity, primarily through home value appreciation, and they want to access all their equity. Since they haven't built 30% or 40% equity, it's very, very difficult to access enough equity to meet their goals with a home equity line of credit. The banks and credit unions won't let you access 100% of the equity in your home like a VA cash-out home loan will allow. It's important to consider the following factors as you evaluate your choices for borrowing. Review how much money you really need, vs. what it's going to cost, vs. what your current VA loan rate and loan balance, are vs. your available equity.

Once you've exhausted your possibilities of a VA cash-out home loan on your first mortgage or a home equity line of credit as a second mortgage, you may want to consider a home improvement loan or installment debt. If you are looking at home improvement projects, these can be reasonable financing options. You may be getting offers from home improvement contractors for installment financing, especially solar system providers. Be very cautious regarding "Hero" (Pace) loans connected to your tax assessment. Currently, nearly all lenders will not finance a first mortgage if one of these loans is attached to your tax assessment. This will prevent buyers from obtaining a loan to purchase your home, if you decide to sell. It will also prevent you from refinancing your VA home loan.

Additionally, I would really caution you to stay away from the "finance companies." I won't name companies here, but their predecessors were Household Finance and Beneficial Finance. "HFC" and "Benne", as they were called, built huge businesses by making small, very high rate second mortgages, and then they went door to door every month collecting payments! Finance companies could be described as any alternative lender, other than traditional banks, credit unions, and mortgage companies. They would typically make loans under $50,000.

From my observation and experience, just the appearance of finance companies on your credit profile is going to depress your credit risk scores overtime. It's a difficult claim to prove, since the Fair Isaac Company will never release the guts of the FICO score(s) formula. If they did, consumers would manipulate their behavior to produce improved scores, thereby rendering the scoring model useless. FICO scores dominate credit decisions and loan pricing, so they are VERY useful and effective in evaluating consumers' likelihood of repaying their debts.

Fair Isaac Company developed the science of credit modeling to determine the probability of default on any particular loan. Their product, your FICO credit risk score, is the result of a proprietary, formulaic review of dozens of your personal financial variables to arrive at an educated guess regarding your ability to repay debts in a timely manner. One of the variables in the formula, which has input into your credit risk scores, examines what kind of credit you have applied for and been approved for in the past. In my experience, people who tend to have lower credit risk scores will often take advantage of credit offers from companies like Roadloans.com, Capitol One, or other companies that market to and service consumers at the lower end of the score spectrum. These types of companies are like the modern day Household Finance or Beneficial Finance. We see finance companies on credit reports somewhat frequently, and again, they are typically associated with lower credit risk score borrowers. There's certainly a need for clients in that credit profile to access credit offerings, but when clients take frequent advantage of these credit offers over time, they almost prevent themselves from raising their credit scores over time. The mere existence of one or more of these finance companies on someone's credit report seems to be profiled by the FICO model and ultimately aides in keeping this profile of consumer's scores depressed. Again, this is just an observation from twenty four years of experience in the loan business, most of which has been dominated by credit risk scoring.

I really encourage clients to stay away from the finance companies and installment debt offered by any companies except banks and credit unions. These credit offerings from finance companies will typically fit in a situation where there's little or no equity in your property. In a scenario where you might need $5,000 - $20,000, an unsecured installment contract may work best. And *when ALL THOSE OTHER options are exhausted,* credit cards are going to be your only remaining option as it pertains to trying to get home improvement projects done.

In conclusion, if you can qualify for it, if you have enough equity, if your credit score is high enough, if you don't want *all* of the equity out of your property, your home equity line of credit is going to be your best bet. It's typically cost-free. It's quick. It's revolving so you can draw on it and pay it down, again and again. However, if you are you're receiving disability from the VA, and therefore are exempt from the VA funding fee, your VA cash-out refinance is a fantastic way to borrow money, as long as the new rate isn't too much higher than your current rate. I'm a big fan of borrowing "cheap money" if you're going to utilize it judiciously and responsibly. If you are not exempt, and you do have to pay the VA funding fee, know that a new loan at a slightly higher than market rate can cover a substantial amount of the closing costs, including some or all of the VA funding fee. As an example, if available interest rates are 4.00% – 5.00% for VA loans, the higher 5.00% rate would offer the opportunity to cover all of the closing costs and absorb nearly all of the VA funding fee expense. The higher rate could very well be a good option because nearly all of the closing costs would be paid for by the lender, leaving more cash out for you!

For assistance on determining which option is best for you, let SoCalVAHomes help. Call us at 888-556-2018.

Chapter 23: The TRUTH About HERO loans

*An in depth examination of the benefits and pitfalls of this new
home improvement financing gadget*

Background

The HERO loan is a "private label" for a PACE loan. They
are the same thing. The concept of the PACE (Property Assessed
Clean Energy) program began in northern California, in San
Francisco in 2001 and in the Monterey Bay in 2005. California
passed the first piece of legislation or PACE financing and started
the Berkeley FIRST climate program in 2008. Since 2008,
legislation enabling PACE programs have now been passed in
more than 31 states. The legislation is popular because it allows
for bond financing for the
purpose of immediately
paying for energy efficient
improvements to commercial
and residential properties.

As it relates to residential property, the distinct difference
between a PACE loan and other secured liens on the home is that
legislation allows the PACE loan to become part of the property
tax assessment. Since property taxes take priority over first
mortgages in a foreclosure, PACE loans are referred to as "super-
superior liens." When a homeowner accepts this financing option,
the new loan just "slips right under" the first mortgage and saddles
up next to the property tax assessment! This is legal, and mortgage
lenders are not too happy about it because it increases their risk of
loss. Should the property fall into foreclosure and get sold,
delinquent property taxes and the PACE loan would get paid first.
Then the lender would be 3rd in line to eventually receive their

share.

PACE loans, or tax assessments, are said to be a debt on the house, not a debt of the homeowner. Unlike a homeowner's mortgage and home equity line that would absolutely have to be paid off during a home sale, the PACE obligation stays with the house. This could potentially encourage homeowners to make immediate improvements rather than hold off because they are uncertain about how long they will own the home and whether they will recoup their investment in the home.

Cisco DeVries is the godfather and inventor of the PACE loan, according to Renew Financial, a company he runs in Oakland, CA. However, the king of the hill appears to be a Notre Dame grad named J.P McNeill, who helps run Renovate America out of San Diego. This company has been the most aggressive marketer of any loan I've seen since the 125% loan, which allowed a homeowner to borrow more than their home was worth. Using the popular NFL quarterback Dan Marino as their TV pitchman, First Plus became the dominant player in the 125% loan market, before it crashed.

In walks The HERO

Renovate America has private labeled their PACE loan calling it the "Award-Winning HERO™ Program," which stands for Home Energy Renovation Opportunity (HERO). This company appears to be dominating the market. From public records and online interviews, it appears they have raised at least $148,959,090 in unregistered securities offerings. In an interview published on cleantechies.com, they appear to be generating a 4.75% securitized return on that capital. That would technically represent the investors return on the money they raised. They are charging their homeowners from 6.75% into the 8.00% range. That doesn't calculate the A.P.R. (Annual Percentage Rate) either, which is much higher, thanks to HERO administration program costs and other fees. Presumably, their gross profit margins before operating costs would be the difference between the 4.75% and the average A.P.R. on their loans – pretty healthy gross margins!

The advantages that the HERO front line sales mechanism presents:

The primary distribution channel of PACE / HERO loans is through home improvement contractors. The clients I have worked with have received sales presentations in their homes from these contractors. One of the advantages of the PACE / HERO program presented by the contractor's sales force would certainly be the outright ability to easily qualify for the loan. HERO loan qualifications have no credit score requirement. Therefore, homeowners with lower credit scores, who may not qualify for other financing alternatives, may be able to qualify for a PACE / HERO loan. That can certainly be viewed as an advantage if you don't have the cash to pay for solar panels or a new roof or other energy efficient home improvements.

Another advantage presented would be the tax advantage. As with mortgage financing, the ability to itemize and deduct the interest (along with your property taxes) on your tax returns might be considered a big advantage, especially for those homeowners in slightly higher tax brackets. Because of the PACE loan's "attachment" to the home's property taxes, effectively integrating the entire loan and its repayment into the property tax payments, a PACE loan appears attractive compared to other forms of financing that have no current effect on a homeowner's income taxes.

Some might even make a far reaching comparison of the

mortgage interest deduction vs. the PACE loan property tax assessment (deduction). Some might conclude that not only is the interest tax-deductable, but so is the principal repayment as well, which is not the case with a mortgage. Unlike a mortgage company that always sends a year-end Form 1098 "mortgage interest paid" statement for tax purposes, HERO loan borrowers do not receive any similar year-end statement. They are left with only their closing documentation and annual property tax bills as ammunition for tax preparation.

Intuit, the software giant that sells the Turbo Tax software, has this to say on its website regarding HERO loan tax deductions, "According to page 151 of IRS Publication No. 17, the principal portion of the payment is deductible for repairs, but not for improvements." On many projects, I could imagine this distinction getting a little fuzzy at tax time. Will this set up borrowers for a potential IRS audit problem, or will it serve as a bigger tax advantage used by borrowers and CPAs? The answer appears unclear and without case history.

Furthermore, the tax assessment and payments facilitate an amortized payment plan that will pay off the lien during the defined term, so lots of principal reduction is included in the annual assessment (payments). This theory of utilizing principal payments in the tax deduction may be a stretch in some circumstances but not without precedent.

When Mello Roos assessments first entered the picture over two decades ago, the real estate community cautioned homeowners about deducting the Mello Roos portion of tax payments on their tax returns. Everyone I have ever encountered did take those deductions, even though they are technically a very small portion of a bond payment. Those bond payments obviously include principal and amortize as well. Technically, the homeowner is getting a deduction on the principal reduction component of the payment, whereas that is not the case with a mortgage payment, where only the interest is tax deductable. I'm not aware of any negative consequences from declaring those deductions. Be advised, we are not offering tax advice, so be sure to consult your tax professional on this matter.

Another "advantage" presented by the contractors could be that the obligation or assessment stays with the property, so it can technically be transferred to the new owner. (However, there might be some serious issues with this assumption!) This aspect of the financing may appeal to homeowners who have an unclear time frame about how long they intend to own the home. If they are undecided about staying in the home long enough to recoup their investment in the project, this potential benefit might be tipping point that facilitates the sale, especially with solar panels which are so popular.

Again, PACE / HERO loans are primarily sold by home improvement contractors. In many of the cases my clients have been involved in, the sales process was initiated by a "door to door" solicitation, generating their interest to pursue a home improvement project. This tactic  represents an "old school," direct sales scenario, almost similar to the days of selling vacuum cleaners door to door to stay-at-home house wives. This practice certainly wouldn't occur in a gated, million dollar home community, where solicitors can't enter and buying decisions often occur without the help of a salesman and with thorough online research ahead of time.

As a contractor, if you're going to send "door knockers" into the field, you would want to use tools and products that would generate the maximum amount of business. The PACE / HERO program works like a charm and "sells like hot-cakes" in neighborhoods with entry level priced homes and homeowners who may not have perfect credit. This is also our market! Active military families and Veterans using their VA home loan benefit to buy homes are very often first time home buyers who don't have perfect credit. These contractors appear to be targeting "FHA & VA neighborhoods."

I have a tremendous respect for the sales profession and the complicated process of moving goods and services from point A to point B. Frankly, everybody sells. Infants begin selling to their mother from birth and perfect those skills through their youth as they ask for what they want and argue their case as teenagers! I have a pretty clear understanding of how these home improvement sales scenarios utilizing HERO loans play out in real time. It can be easy to generate interest and more convenient to sell benefits to a customer in need when only the "surface level" advantages are presented. Often the disadvantages are not mentioned, and the customer is on their own to discover the pitfalls of their decision after the sale.

Disadvantages of the PACE / HERO financing sales mechanism

There are several disadvantages of this product and its distribution system. As a homeowner with a PACE / HERO loan attached to the home, you can't utilize conventional financing to refinance, and your buyers can not use it to purchase, which may stop a home sale. Many FHA & VA lenders have also adopted the same position, declining loan applications on homes with a PACE / HERO loan attached. In addition to those show stoppers, the interest rates and fees are relatively high, compared to other secured lien mortgage products.

Unfortunately, in 100% of the cases that I have evaluated with my clients, the borrowers were not truly informed of all the long-term consequences of accepting a PACE / HERO loan to finance their home improvement projects. They also didn't spend the time to compare financing options on their projects. In addition, they thought that there was no effect at all on their opportunity to refinance. And they were not aware of any effect that the PACE / HERO loan may have on the future sale of their property.

Because the main distribution channel for HERO loans seems to be through contractors, this sales mechanism can result in surprises to the homeowner. Renovate America partners with contactors and offers them "exclusive discounts and rebates," so they can "close more deals," according to the website. The business model is terrific, and I applaud its success, but the homeowners need to be made aware of the potential consequences of their financing decision during the sales process.

During the sales presentation, contractors are primarily focusing on selling their company and the benefits of their home improvements to the homeowners. After that portion of their presentation, they sprinkle the "sugar on top," selling the features or advantages of the HERO loan, such as easy qualifying and tax benefits. From the standpoint of selling benefits to the homeowner, the contractors have been handed a terrific new "tool in their box." Selling a home improvement project just got easier with no credit requirements and enhanced tax benefits! *It's not surprising that the contractors leave the disadvantages out of the sales pitch.*

Many products that contractors are selling fill a need in an emergency, such as heating and air conditioning or a new roof, perhaps before the winter rains. Naturally, homeowners are looking for a way to solve their emergency problem quickly, as opposed to giving a lot of consideration to financing alternatives.

And typically, the homeowner who needs financing as opposed to paying cash for a repair is the homeowner with a lower credit profile. And the same homeowner with lower credit scores is going to be a better prospect for a PACE / HERO loan.

Disadvantages of the PACE / HERO financing product

As I stated, you'll have potential problems with any new financing on the home, and PACE / HERO rates and fees are high. There is a significant amount of back story on this problem that could put you to sleep with the detail. Included in the back story are colorful events such as a lawsuit filed on whether the agencies Fannie Mae and Freddie Mac had the right to decline financing on properties with PACE / HERO loans. California Governor Jerry Brown sued the Federal Housing Finance Agency (FHFA) to overturn its decision support the agencies' position. In 2013, a federal appeals court upheld the Agency's right to prevent the government sponsored enterprises (GSEs), Fannie Mae and Freddie Mac, from buying loans involved in this program.

FHFA was established by the Housing and Economic Recovery Act of 2008 (HERA) and is responsible for the effective supervision, regulation, and oversight of the Federal National Mortgage Association (Fannie Mae), the Federal Home Loan Mortgage Corporation (Freddie Mac), and the Federal Home Loan Bank System. They essentially play "mortgage king" overseeing a majority of our real estate financing system.

After PACE loans became popular in California, primarily through the aggressive marketing from Renovate America to promote their HERO program, a decision was rendered and announced by the FHFA. Below is the conclusion of their position and a statement (WARNING) to homeowners considering PACE / HERO financing:

STATEMENT OF THE FEDERAL HOUSING FINANCE AGENCY (FHFA) ON CERTAIN SUPER-PRIORITY LIENS

FOR IMMEDIATE RELEASE

12/22/2014

In issuing this statement, FHFA wants to make clear to homeowners, lenders, other financial institutions, state officials, and the public that Fannie Mae and Freddie Mac's policies prohibit the purchase of a mortgage where the property has a first-lien PACE loan attached to it. This restriction has two potential implications for borrowers. First, a homeowner with a first-lien PACE loan cannot refinance their existing mortgage with a Fannie Mae or Freddie Mac mortgage. Second, anyone wanting to buy a home that already has a first-lien PACE loan cannot use a Fannie Mae or Freddie Mac loan for the purchase. These restrictions may reduce the marketability of the house or require the homeowner to pay off the PACE loan before selling the house.

FHFA believes it is important for states and municipalities to understand these restrictions before continuing to offer the programs. **Additionally, FHFA believes that borrowers should fully understand these restrictions prior to taking out a first-lien PACE loan.**

As you can see from the statement, the "800 lb. gorillas" in the mortgage marketplace have taken a strong position regarding PACE / HERO loans. If for any reason a property suffers a foreclosure, Fannie's and Freddie's lien position, and therefore their security, is compromised with a PACE / HERO loan on the home. So the FHFA has opted out! But what about the government loans, FHA & VA?

More disadvantages to PACE / HERO loans: FHA and VA lenders choose sides

Ultimately, a process known as securitization drives mortgage lenders' guidelines regarding how to package home loans. Since Lew Ranieri of Solomon Brothers invented mortgage-backed securities more than three decades ago, lenders sell loans to Fannie Mae, Freddie Mac and GNMA (pronounced "Ginniemae"), the Government National Mortgage Association. These three buyers make up a large majority of the mortgage loan volume in the U.S. Lenders sell mortgage loans to these agencies and replenish their capital. These agencies aggregate (securitize) billions of dollars in loans together, and they sell the payment streams to institutional investors, replenishing their capital.

While FNMA and FHLMC purchase the conventional loans, GNMA purchases nearly 100% of FHA and VA loans. GNMA provides lenders basic underwriting guidelines of how to package these loans. FHA mortgage insurance and the VA Loan Guaranty Certificate work very differently in how they provide lender protections against loss due to foreclosure. Therefore, the underwriting guidelines to prepare an individual loan for funding and sale to GNMA differ from FHA to VA. On top of that, lenders must manage risk in their own individual ways, as they see fit. As we have witnessed, it's a risky business. Remember all the foreclosures from the financial crisis of 2008? Lenders lost billions. Let's now briefly examine the history of how FHA and VA lenders address a property when a PACE / HERO loan enters the picture. How does this affect you, the homeowner?

July 19, 2016, FHA Mortgagee Letter 2016-11: FHA has provided "clear guidance" regarding this tricky topic. "Properties which will remain encumbered with a PACE obligation may be eligible for FHA-insured mortgage financing, provided that the mortgagee determines that the following requirements have been met." While the details of this policy are tedious, the story unfolds in an interesting manner.

July 19, 2016, the Department of Veterans Affairs, Circular 26-16-18: The VA states an identical position, including:

"b. The property may be subject to the full PACE obligation; however, the property shall not be subject to an enforceable claim (i.e., a lien) superior to the VA-guaranteed loan for the full outstanding PACE obligation at any time.

c. The property may, however, be subject to an enforceable claim (i.e., a lien) that is superior to the VA-guaranteed loan for delinquent regularly scheduled PACE special assessments. (Note: If VA acquires ownership of a property that is subject to a PACE obligation, or if VA is assigned a VA-guaranteed loan that is secured by such a property, nothing in this policy should be construed as a waiver or release of VA's federal property rights or legal claims related to such property rights.)"

In my opinion, these statements from FHA & VA seriously conflict with the original state legislation that provides for PACE financing. I'm not a real estate attorney, but in a foreclosure, it's not immediately apparent, whose lien is senior. Both parties seem to be making a claim to that position. I think many lenders seem to agree with me, because I have personally surveyed the lenders who buy our loans after they have funded, and a large majority won't touch a FHA or VA loan when a PACE / HERO loan exists on the tax assessment! This doesn't bode well for you as the homeowner trying to sell or refinance when financing options are seriously constricted.

More than a year and a half of pain for our VA borrowers

The VA Loan Guaranty only offers protection for the lender on the first 25% of the loan balance. In that manner, the loan guaranty substitutes for the down payment in a conventional scenario. It reduces the lender's risk, but it doesn't eliminate it altogether. Once the FHFA Statement was issued in December 2014, lenders offering VA loans adjusted their underwriting guidelines prohibiting the existence of PACE loans on the property, effectively eliminating the possibility of our VA borrowers to combine their home loan benefit with PACE on a new VA loan.

As rates continued to drop, legions of VA borrowers responded to lender's solicitations to use VA streamline refinancing (VA IRRRL) guidelines to easily lower their interest rates. Imagine the disappointment of those men and women who served and now had PACE / HERO loan, when a VA loan professional told them, "I'm sorry sir, you're stuck because you got the HERO loan." I was the one making that statement many, many times. That was reality for every VA refinance prospect in that situation.

At that time, if the VA client wanted to take advantage of lower mortgage rates, the PACE / HERO loan would have to be paid off with a larger VA cash-out refinance loan. To qualify, the VA borrower needed adequate credit and enough income to support the larger debt load. They also had to have enough equity to include both the existing first mortgage and the PACE / HERO loan in the new loan balance, not to exceed the new appraised value.

AND HERE IS WHERE IT GOT THE UGLIEST: If the homeowner was not receiving disability payments from the VA (and exempt from paying the VA funding fee), the fee tacked on another 3.3% on top of the of the new base loan amount. And that could be a significant sum to repay. In nearly all cases that I worked with, the HERO loan killed the deal one way or another.

Since July 19th 2016, a limited number of lenders have decided to take the risk and to make FHA and VA financing available, only if the PACE / HERO lender will record a document know as a "Subordination Agreement." This document officially releases the "senior lien claim" of the PACE / HERO loan and purportedly puts the new FHA or VA loan in "first position." Again, a majority of the lenders I work with will not make the loan, but the Renovate America website states that they may subordinate the lien. Again, this is a dicey, grey space without legal precedent. And none of this has been tested in a declining value market. In a declining market with increasing foreclosures, I think this story of opposing interests between FHA / VA lenders and PACE lenders will produce another chapter. As foreclosures potentially mount, the boxing gloves from both opposing entities will undoubtedly appear as each party strives to protect their financial interests.

Disadvantages of PACE / HERO loans when trying to sell your home

If you are trying to sell your house, the existence of a PACE / HERO loan presents problems. What if your buyer wants to use conventional financing? You'll have to pay off the PACE / HERO loan during the closing of the sale. What if the value of your home (including the improvements paid for by the loan) is not enough to allow the PACE / HERO loan to be paid off during the sale? Closing costs to sell the home must also enter the equation. Your sales price must accommodate your mortgage payoff, the PACE / HERO loan payoff and your closing costs. If your sales price is not high enough, you will have to write a check to close the sale. If you can't write the check, you're stuck in the house or looking for another buyer who will use other financing.

Again, if the buyer's lender chooses not to make loans on a home with a PACE / HERO loan attached to the tax assessment, your home buyer won't be able to get financing. You won't be able to sell your house to that buyer!

High interest rates and fees on a PACE / HERO loan

Compared to the old finance companies like Household Finance and Beneficial Finance, PACE / HERO loans are cheap. But those companies are long gone, and compared to current mortgage products, those loans are EXPENSIVE! With rates from 6.75% into the 8.00% range, the HERO loan rates are very high. Currently, that's double the rate of what a first mortgage charges. And the fees are high enough to be illegal, if it was a mortgage product. "QM" (Qualified Mortgage) guidelines require qualifying mortgages to have fees less than 3.0% of the loan amount. "Outdated" CA-AB489 California statutes required mortgage loan fees to be 5.00% or less than the loan amount.

When trying to help clients refinance, I have reviewed HERO documentation demonstrating HERO loan fees between 6.50% - 9.0% of the loan amount. If we use a standard A.P.R. (Annual Percentage Rate) calculation and a comparison, it would be obvious that the high loan fees dramatically increase the cost of borrowing. As an example, on one client's HERO loan that was paid off on 12/5/2016, the HERO loan fees were $1,783.81 on loan proceeds of $19,900. That's a whopping 8.964% of fees on top of the amount that was available for the client to utilize.

On another client's HERO loan that was paid off on 11/28/2016 (using a VA cash-out refi):

- The loan amount proceeds were $42,699, and additional HERO loan fees were $2,793.05.
- The NOTE Rate was 6.50%.
- A 60 month term would result in a payment = $985.44.
- If an A.P.R. were calculated on this data, **it would be 9.44% - that's HIGH!**

That is a "finance company rate," similar to a used car loan for a borrower with a credit score of less than 580. Considering this loan is a "super lien," and extremely well "secured," in my opinion, Renovate America is "killing it," CRUSHING IT…knocking it out of the ball park in every way with their business! Again, my congrats gentlemen.

Well, it is legal. Finance companies, like Household Finance have been doing it to consumers (including Veterans) for literally more than a century. Household Finance used to knock on doors to generate home improvement financing business. Sound familiar? In some cases, providing credit to those borrowers who can't otherwise access credit could be considered a valuable service. As a Veteran, please do your homework to determine if it's right for you.

Paying off a PACE / HERO loan during a refinance...be prepared for surprises

I've paid off a number of HERO loans and it's a huge hassle for everyone, especially the client, and especially during the property tax season when taxes are due. In California, property taxes are due on November 1st and delinquent on December 11th. Estimating the new VA cash-out refinance loan amount and managing the possible property tax refunds from the HERO loan and the county tax assessor's office is difficult for the inexperienced.

You may have to pay your HERO loan property tax assessment THREE TIMES OVER and then have to wait for multiple refunds. It does happen. If the closing of the refinance is in November, and the escrow officer cannot confirm that your current loan servicer has paid the property taxes now due, then the taxes (with the HERO assessment) must be paid through the closing of your refinance. If it's in late November, it's likely that the loan servicer HAS paid the property taxes as well. So they get paid twice. On the second payment received by the county tax assessor's office, they should send the funds back from where they came as the first refund. And it's a BIG one, because it has the HERO assessment included!

It gets worse. The HERO loan administrators will issue a payoff statement for escrow to respond to. That payoff will include not only the principal, but also the interest, administration program cost, county recording, processing and "other fees." In this payoff statement, there exists a significant redundancy of the amount paid in the county tax assessment, which of course includes the HERO loan assessment. If it were not "property tax season," (11/01-12/10), this would be a non-event. The HERO loan would get fully settled – period. But during property tax season, the title company MUST pay the tax assessment due to the county (or confirm that the current loan servicer has paid them) on a refinance per the new lender's instructions. The payoff of the HERO loan doesn't exclude that requirement.

In this circumstance, the county gets their taxes twice and the HERO assessment gets paid THREE times. Follow the money... The payoff from escrow directly to the HERO loan administrators makes the outstanding HERO loan balance zero and pays all the itemized HERO loan fees, most of which were included in the original contract. The county tax assessor's office received two payments for one tax bill, so escrow or the previous loan servicer (the check that was received second by the county) should receive a refund from the county. This refund for the duplicated tax payment (including HERO), must go back to the homeowner. This is the first large refund the client must track. And finally, according to a well trained HERO customer service agent, there's a refund from the HERO loan administrator that must be tracked.

The HERO loan administrator receives a payment from the county which collects the funds as part of the assessment, right? But, the HERO loan has now been paid in full by escrow, so the HERO tax assessment got paid twice. A refund is due to the homeowner who must wait approximately three months to receive it! This is a bit insulting considering the payoff statement from the HERO loan administrator includes interest payable WAY BEYOND the date of payoff, effectively acting as an early payoff fee! The payment from the county gets issued to the bank which handles the cash flow and accounting on the HERO loan's "asset-backed security." This is a block of HERO loans all packaged together. The overpayment of this homeowner's account ultimately gets discovered and then the funds meander their way back to the patient homeowner. WHEW!

Getting the impound account correct on the new VA cash out refinance loan that pays off HERO...a small challenge that creates delays...and the delays don't stop there!

Hopefully your VA loan professional can handle the minor issues! Educating escrow officers, mortgage loan underwriters and loan document preparation clerks is necessary to the successful funding of new loan that pays off a PACE / HERO loan. I have not witnessed one person who subtracted the HERO tax assessment OUT of the new escrow impound account, without a specific request. They look at the title report, see the "excessive tax amount," and without considering that the HERO loan is being paid off, they include the HERO tax assessment in the new impound account and resulting payment. Each time, they need to be reminded to take the HERO assessment back out of the equation. I have even had funding delays because of appraisals being prepared "subject to" the HERO special assessment being paid off. This confused the funder who asked for an additional inspection that wasn't necessary. Paying off these loans is a new process – a hassle!

After PACE / HERO loans get paid off. Are there more problems on the horizon?

Tax assessment and resulting first mortgage loan payment problems may occur for homeowners even after the PACE / HERO loan is paid off. In some circumstances, the tax assessments recorded and continually updated at the county assessor's office likely won't update fast enough for all client circumstances. Imagine this scenario: Using the only available property tax assessment, which is now too large and "outdated" and includes the now paid off PACE / HERO loan, the new loan servicer is likely to overpay the property taxes due February 1st, delinquent April 11th.

They won't have a choice. They will get the "current" tax bill which still includes the PACE / HERO loan assessment, and they will pay it. This will likely create some problems for some clients as their new escrow account on their new loan immediately goes into a deficit and the loan servicer subsequently sends them a letter notifying them of the option to increase their payment or write a check!

Evaluating PACE / HERO loans and their advantages and disadvantages is a complicated process. The decision to use this financing can only be concluded after consulting professionals who truly understand all aspects of this equation. For assistance in making this important decision, feel free to call SoCalVAHomes at 888-556-2018.

Chapter 24: Easily Exchangeable Loans - The VA Streamline Refinance

When Should You Refinance Your VA Home Loan?

The Tremendous Advantages of a VA "IRRRL"

Advertisements for VA loans are everywhere. You hear radio ads, TV commercials, and if you have a VA loan already, your mailbox gets filled every week with solicitations. If rates click down just a notch, there's a massive pile of mail screaming for your attention! Is this stuff for real? There's just an avalanche of it with bold claims of "lower rates." Why does it seem as if having a VA loan makes you a target for solicitors? Where do these people who call you get your number from? Should you respond to any of these offers?

Refinancing, by definition, is simply replacing old financing with new financing (a new mortgage) because the new terms are more favorable to you. In the money game, it's the ultimate do-over, a second (or third or fourth…) chance to take advantage of a new opportunity. Homeowners with VA home loans consider refinancing for a variety of reasons, including to obtain a better interest rate, to reduce monthly payments, to consolidate debts by paying off credit cards, or to free-up cash, often for home improvements. There are four reasons to refinance:

- You have a fixed rate and lower rates are now available (e.g., if you have a 5% loan and 4% is now available). Such a "refi" is considered a <u>fixed rate to fixed rate.</u>
- If you have an <u>adjustable loan</u> and want the security of a fixed rate loan. Often in this case, people were enticed by the really low start rate that was offered, and now they want to go back to a fixed rate.
- Some people have a fixed rate but want the lower payments that are available on an adjustable loan. Such a refi is called a <u>fixed to adjustable.</u>
- If someone wants a <u>cash-out refinance</u>, typically where the homeowner's property has appreciated (e.g., the property was purchased for 400K three years ago and the property values went up 25% so now it is worth 500K), and you want to take out funds for home improvements, debt consolidation or other reasons. (See Chapter 22: *The Cash-Out VA Refinance vs. An Equity Line* for in-depth detail on financing options.)

Homeowners who purchase a home using their VA Home Loan Benefit often don't understand the compelling reasons to refinance. They may be skeptical of all the solicitations. Or they may have had a bad experience getting their purchase loan. Or they maintain a stubborn stance because they simply don't want to "start all over again" with a new loan because their goal is to pay off the debt, pure and simple. This is the biggest mistake. There are a host of reasons creating resistance when it comes to refinancing and preventing our men and women who serve from taking advantage of a bona fide, legitimate opportunity to achieve better terms on a new loan. This is especially true as it pertains to a "fixed rate to fixed rate" refinance.

It's very common for a buyer to purchase a property with a

fixed rate and then come up with a list of objections as to why they will not refinance to a lower rate. Unfortunately, many of these objections are "self-invented myths" that prevent our VA borrowers from improving their financial situation. Often the improvements can be life changing with respect to properly managing their finances.

This situation is very familiar to us at SoCalVAHomes. We have tracked the data and seen the evidence. There exists a group of about 5000 home owners with VA loans across the state of California who bought their homes between 2007 and July of 2011. This specific group of VA borrowers all have the same original financing. They still have the same purchase loan that helped them buy the house. During that time, 30 year fixed rates averaged about 5.50%. Since that time frame, rates dropped to as low as 3.00%. For the years between 2011 - 2015, "no points, no fees" refinance opportunities existed at 3.75%. There has been more than enough opportunities for at least some of those 5000 VA borrowers to take advantage of lower rates, yet they don't. We're certain it's not a matter of these homeowners qualifying to get approved for a better loan. They just are not taking action. These home owners with VA loans could truly benefit from a new loan with a much lower rate, without raising their loan balance or incurring any closing costs. The opportunity is actually far MORE compelling than just a lower rate achieved without incurring any costs at all. And yet, over the years, this is what we hear from clients when they initially call:

"It's too much of a hassle."

"I'll have to write a check up front or at closing."

"I disliked my previous loan office/mortgage company."

"My grandfather told me the rate needs to be at least 2% lower."

"I don't understand or trust the process, and I'm skeptical of all the solicitors."

"I find the whole thing intimidating."

"It's too much paperwork."

"It costs too much."

"My transaction costs were $10,000 – there's no way I'm paying that again."

"My loan balance goes up."

"I need equity, or my house is 'upside down.' I owe more than it's worth."

"I'm retired and won't qualify." "I changed jobs." "I'm self-employed."

"I don't want my property taxes to go up."

"I need an attorney to review all the papers, and I can't afford one."

"My credit's not good enough."

This list of roadblocks goes on and on. But the most financially debilitating or damaging "opinion" or feeling from many homeowners is this:

> *"It was so much effort and cost to get that loan! And it seems that I just did it.....I feel like I'm losing out and not taking full advantage of the loan I got if I replace it with a new loan."*

There is a strong emotional attachment to the effort and/or expense which produced a loan that is NOW OBSOLETE.   I totally understand this feeling. However, the inability to release yourself from that gripping emotional attachment and the resulting paralysis and lack of action can have serious financial consequences. Not refinancing when the opportunity presents itself is simply financially foolish. This INACTION is perhaps the most financially damaging and irresponsible choice that a Veteran can make. Unfortunately, it is too common.

A NO POINTS, NO FEES, NO COST VA LOAN REFINANCE IS A "FREE" LOAN.

Here's how the transaction can be constructed to get a new loan for "free" that actually PAYS YOU to take advantage of an offer. No loan is ever "free." However, accepting a "higher rate" than lower rate alternatives typically allows the lender to absorb all the closing costs without raising your new loan balance. An escrow impound account can be refunded to you from your old lender while the closing costs can include a new impound account and two months of interest. You effectively bypass two months of payments and get an impound account refund. Here's how it all works "underneath the surface".

Save Money
with a No Cost Mortgage

If you're not taking any cash out (you are only reducing your fixed rate or replacing an adjustable VA loan with a fixed rate), your transaction is called a VA streamline refinance. In lender's terms, it is called an Interest Rate Reduction Refinance Loan or IRRRL. It is typically the easiest loan to qualify for among all loan applications. Very little is required from a client to produce the result.

Lenders can literally construct a no-points, no-fees 30 year fixed rate loan program, without your loan balance going up above your current principal balance. When funded, your new loan balance will be the same as your old loan balance. As an example, imagine you've got a $300,000 loan at 5.00%, and rates have dropped allowing new choices of rates between 3.75% - 4.50%. When you choose the rate of 4.50% (obviously the rate at high end of the range), special things can happen for you. Here's how the math makes a "free" loan work for all parties. First, you'll pay 0.50% less in interest for the life of the loan, and it didn't cost you anything. Your initial reaction may be skeptical because you ask, "What's in it for the new lender? How do they get paid?" Good question. Here's how.

At the highest end of the available interest rate range (4.50% vs. 3.75% in this example), a large sum of money is available to pay for closing costs and provide enough for the lender to earn a reasonable profit. These funds are universally available to distribute to all parties in the transaction, including the lender and the lender's loan officer. More importantly, funds are available to the borrower to pay for all the typical closing costs, including funding the new impound account for taxes and insurance as well as interest to bridge the gap between the old loan and the new loan. These funds are not available when choosing the lowest rate options. Here's WHERE the funds come from.

If you're an investor, you'll be happy to advance a measured sum of money, literally pay some money UP FRONT, for the opportunity to receive a higher yield / higher rate of return on your investment and larger distributions or larger regular payments to you for the life of the investment. As an investor, you PAY a little up front and get a bigger return in the long run. This investor is known as GNMA – the Government National Mortgage Association. The loan is sold by the lender and purchased by

GNMA. GNMA facilitates the "secondary loan market" by placing your loan into a GNMA investment security with thousands of other loans. GNMA then sells these securities or investments to "institutional investors" such as large insurance companies. Through this process, there's plenty of money that is "advanced" through the "loan food chain," into your loan closing to pay for closing costs, when you choose the higher rate!

If you select a lower rate, the yield or rate of return to the investor drops. These funds available for your closing costs disappear as you slide down the scale of rate choices for your new loan. In the "lower rate" scenario, the lack of these available funds translate into an increased loan balance as closing costs are financed, or simply added to the new loan balance.

Again, when you've selected the higher rate, and as the transaction funds, money flows forward from the lender into your escrow account (at the title company). Because these funds pay for your closing costs, the loan balance does not need to be increased as it would with a "higher-rate" choice where these funds are not available.

The actual lender gets repaid on the advance of the funds when the loan is immediately sold into a GNMA security - the investment. The sum of money achieved by the loan sale to GNMA (to pay for all this at the highest rate) is substantial. The loan sale can achieve as much as five points or more. That's 5% more than the principal loan balance. On a $100,000 loan, the lender can receive $5,000 or more. That's how "mortgage banking" functions. It can be a substantial sum of money that can then be allocated from all of your closing costs and still result in some left over so the mortgage company can remain profitable. Recall that there are no VA non-profit lenders. VA lending is a for profit universe in which the participants take substantial risks within their businesses. The VA does not make loans. It only provides the 25% VA Guaranty to partially cover the lender's risk of foreclosure. And VA loans default at a substantially more frequent pace than conventional loans.

The Highlights and Benefits of the "Free" VA Loan

- **No added loan balance:** Because you have chosen the higher rate option, your loan balance has not increased, and your new loan is properly budgeted to pay your property tax liabilities, your insurance premiums and the interest due to both the old lender and new.

- **Skipping two payments:** When two months of interest is included in the transaction, you will bypass two mortgage payments. Those funds stay in your checking account. There is no effect on your good credit as long as your old loan is paid off and credited to the old lender on or before the last day of the month in which you held back your final payment. Interest then accrues in the following month after funding your new loan. This results in your first payment due on the new loan on the 1st of the following month after funding. Again, you bypass two payments. That is the "cherry on top" of this refinance!

- **Escrow impound account refund:** Because you have chosen the higher rate option, your new impound account has been funded with the lender's money, not yours. What has become of your previous escrow impound account with your previous loan servicer? Those funds were always yours and were set aside to pay for your taxes and insurance.

- When the previous loan was paid off, it triggered and audit by the previous loan servicer. If your old escrow impound account was running a deficit at payoff, no refund is due. This is a rarity. If that was the case, your old payment was about to be raised to cover the deficit. If there existed a "surplus" in your escrow impound account, then these surplus funds must be returned to you promptly, usually within 30 days of pay off. Escrow impound accounts are typically budgeted to operate at a surplus, so a refund to you is common on a VA refinance.

Even if the change in interest rate only results in a relatively small reduction in payment, the cost is only measured in your time spent, and the return on your invested time is ENORMOUS. Consider spending about two hours to receive these benefits measured in thousands of dollars:

- No money out of pocket.
- A new loan balance equal to your current loan balance.
- A lower 30 Year Fixed Rate mortgage payment.
- Bypass two months of payments (with no affect to your good credit).
- A substantial impound account refund from your current lender.

Take advantage of all the benefits discussed in this chapter and let SoCalVAHomes help. Call us at 888-556-2018.

Chapter 25: The Energy Efficient Mortgage

Your VA Home Loan Benefit Offers $6000 for Energy Efficient Home Improvements. Why?

Active military and Veterans often call lenders looking for a way to lower their monthly mortgage payment. The main method or loan product to lower your interest rate, which then lowers your monthly payment of your VA home loan, is called an IRRRL or an Interest Rate Reduction Refinance Loan. This aspect of your Veteran's benefit allows you to refinance your VA mortgage to a lower rate VA mortgage.

An Energy Efficient Mortgage (EEM), is a component to the new loan which can be applied for at the same time that you're applying for a VA streamline refinance, also known as an Interest Rate Reduction Refinance Loan (IRRRL, pronounced "Earl"). So the EEM component is icing on the cake when applying for the IRRRL.

In the EEM version of the IRRRL loan, there is a component

Energy efficient mortgage

that allows for an extra $6000 cash-out, over and above the new loan balance. The VA EEM enables you to purchase new energy efficient home improvements. This may include things that would reduce your heating or A/C bill like double pane windows or solar panels (usually a bit more than $6000!) These funds are not a gift or grant! Because you borrow it, the loan amount increases. But you don't need to further qualify for the additional $6000 in any way. Still, your extra $6000 is not cash that you are free and clear to spend as you see fit. The money *has* to be applied towards energy efficient home improvements.

Borrowers either like or altogether disregard this feature of the VA streamline refinance. For some people, this extra $6000 simply isn't worth the trouble. Again, to receive the $6000, you must agree to purchase things that conserve energy such as double-paned windows or even technology like LED light bulbs! But you are also required to follow some rules which may be too restrictive for you. You have to:

- Hire a contractor for all home improvement elements.
- Have the contractor vetted and approved by the lender.
- Disburse the funds through the escrow account (usually at a title company) which handled the funding of the entire refinance.

Essentially, the $6000 needs to be parceled out from the escrow account as the contractor invoices the completed projects. This process is known as a contractor "draw" from escrow.

This cumbersome process can add months to closing your "streamline" refinance! It can seriously delay the process of getting a lower interest rate, while you fret over the extra $6000. The significant delay can also create havoc with the rate locking strategy for the lender. Your opportunity for a lower rate could actually disappear, should rates rise during the extra time involved to fund the EEM streamline refinance. Most loans are locked for only fifteen, thirty, even sixty days at the very longest, and it can take that long, PLUS sixty days, to make sure that you qualify the EEM job by getting your bids, submitting them, qualifying the contractor, getting the approval, etc.

The EEM IRRRL or EEM streamline refinance is something that is advertised, but it is rarely taken advantage of due to all the hoops that you have to jump through to utilize the additional $6.000. Therefore, very few lenders seriously offer it on their menu of loan products.

Additionally, there is another "financial windfall" for the borrower on an IRRRL, which seems to replace the desire for the benefits of an EEM IRRRL. All VA loans require an escrow impound account, budgeted for property tax and insurance payments. The refinance and pay off of that loan can easily produce a refund in that impound account paid directly to the homeowner/borrower, which is perceived as a big benefit! This amount can be substantial for a homeowner with significant annual property taxes, especially when the transaction closes right before taxes are to be paid, when the account is at its highest levels. Add to that the ability to finance sixty days of interest into ANY refinance, and thereby bypass two mortgage payments, and you can now accumulate a tidy sum into your checking account when these two sums of money are added together! In comparison, when the $6000 is considered as an EEM vs. the escrow account refund paid directly to you, plus bypassing two loan payments on the typical IRRRL, many prospective applicants will just ditch the idea of the EEM.

However, for some, especially when the $6000 is a relatively large sum, energy efficiency is well-worth the extra effort. Some of these home improvement energy technologies are pretty cool. If you have work to do on your home, why not go ahead and install some of the latest tech toys and state-of-the-art materials to create a more comfortable, "green" home? Energy efficiency devices and materials that are acceptable under these mortgage guidelines include, but are not limited to:

- Thermal storm windows and doors.
- Solar water heater.
- Efficiency insulation for water heaters.
- Permanent air conditioning.

- Vapor barriers.
- Heat pumps.
- Wall, floor, ceiling and attic insulation.
- Caulking and weather stripping.
- LED lightbulbs.

Not only will you be cooler in the summer and warmer in the winter, you will achieve the benefit of long term savings simply by not being wasteful. Green homes are increasingly popular, not just as a smart investment, but also because they fit with the deeply held American value of environmental conservation.

If you are interested in any additional information on home improvements or what qualifies as an Energy Efficient Home Improvement, let SoCalVAHomes help. Call us at 888-556-2018.

Chapter 26: Mission Control Center

Fundamental Financial Planning for Veterans and Military Families

DISCLAIMER: *The information contained herein is for educational purposed only. Consult an investment advisor and/or a CPA for tax and investment advice prior to investing. The author and or his affiliates are as such not responsible for the reader's tax disposition/liability or the merits of any investment strategies.*

This chapter is primarily focused on those Veterans who will not have military careers which result in military retirement pay that will support their retirement lifestyle. A large majority of our servicemen and  women will not receive any retirement pay (or qualify for any VA disability benefit) to support themselves after their discharge. You'll have to plan for your retirement in the same way civilians do!

If you have ever had money problems, or just can't seem to save and invest much, you are not alone. Unfortunately, financial literacy is not usually taught in school, not taught in most homes, and not taught in depth in the military. Financial discipline, the act of deploying financial literacy, is a "muscle group" that you must discover, explore and exercise on your own. Like most subjects, the school of hard knocks is the teacher.

Fundamental financial planning is really just financial common sense mixed with some easy to learn information and discipline in your investing habits. There are three easy steps to create financial well-being and even wealth. It's not what you earn it's what you *save*!

- Save.
- Establish an emergency fund.
- Invest, early and consistently.

Saving

One way to quickly and easily begin to save and invest may be to utilize your VA loan benefit to buy a home. YOU have this amazing tool at your disposal! You have the unique advantage of being able to purchase or "leverage" real estate at 100% of the price of the home because you can get real estate financing with a VA loan.

As a homeowner, *you are building equity* because as you make loan payments, you are reducing your principal balance. Assuming your property value doesn't decline, you are building value each month in your investment. (Equity equals the value of your home or property minus whatever remaining loan balance you have.) Your house is, in essence, an automatic savings program (as long as properties aren't depreciating). Your "real estate" savings program is increasing in value every time you make a mortgage payment. It's literally a forced savings plan, creating wealth through your home.

As an owner you can also build wealth through appreciation, a common investment strategy. Of course, in most cases, there are tax advantages from your mortgage interest deduction and your property tax deduction. All of the above are tremendous benefits that you should take advantage of, if you are in the right spot in your life to be a property owner, not a renter.

Be aggressive with your savings amounts. If you are a terrible saver, you are not alone. Americans typically save somewhere between 2% and 6% of their gross income. That may not get you the kind of retirement you want. Following these fundamental financial planning "Golden Rules" will earn you the "golden ticket" to the "golden years!"

Let's demonstrate some examples of why it's important to begin saving as early as possible and remain consistent in your savings discipline.

INVESTOR 1, starting at age 20, contributes $200/month @ 8.00% annual yield* for 20 years. The total accumulation value of this investment would be = $117,804. This investor then stops contributing and lets it "ride" for 20 more years. This investment then grows to a total value of $580,397. I can't emphasize enough how important it is to begin saving early in life. A $580,397 retirement nest egg was accumulated with only $200/month x 240 payments for a total of $48,000. Compounding returns over a long time period is what produces the greatest results.

INVESTOR 2 contributes $200/month @ 8.00% annual yield* for 40 years. The total accumulation value of this investment would be $698,201.

INVESTOR 3 contributes $200/month @ 10.00% annual yield* for 40 years. The total accumulation value of this investment would be = $1,264,816,

INVESTOR 4contributes $200/month @ 12.00% annual yield* for 40 years. The total accumulation value of this investment would be = $2,352,954.

Note: The previous examples demonstrate the need to be aggressive in search of higher yields. Small incremental changes in yields produce HUGE results when compounded over time!

INVESTOR 5 contributes $458/month @ 12.00% annual yield* for 40 years. The total accumulation value of this investment would be = $5,392,187. This demonstrates the necessity of saving and investing a significant portion of your income.

*Yields are compounded monthly with tax deferred growth, as in an IRA or 401k. In 2014 – 2015, IRA contribution limits were set at $5,500 or $458/month and $6,500 if you're age 50 or older. Tax "advantaged" growth is always an objective.

"Average Stock Market Returns," are supported with lots of data. Without debating methods of calculations and possible inconsistencies, the data suggests that average stock market returns or "yields" fall somewhere between 7.5% - $12.00%. Without making an investment and letting it appreciate for decades, or without consistently adding to your investment, you won't experience "averaged" returns of the long haul. Again, time and consistency are your friends here, and a technique called "dollar cost averaging" is achieved by utilizing both time and consistency.

Dollar cost averaging

This is simply a mathematical argument for achieving consistency in investment purchase prices over time. By consistently investing the same amount, at the same time intervals, you avoid the typically futile attempt of "timing" your purchases of mutual fund shares or another investment. It can be nearly impossible to guess "market lows," hoping to buy at low points and then sell at high points. Don't bother guessing! Many smart novice investors make consistent monthly contributions, "dollar cost averaging" their share price of their purchases, by investing every month at a "low" price or a "high" price. Over time this can produce a very satisfactory "average" purchase price as the general stock market rises.

The message from these examples and simple mathematical data is intended to prove only one single point. You can get rich and retire wealthy...ANYONE CAN. It just takes executing the fundamentals of investing early and staying consistent.

Pay Yourself First

Making a commitment to save a significant percentage of your income every payday, right off the top of your paycheck, is how you pay yourself first. Saving BEFORE you make purchases for living expenses or discretionary items is the only strategy that absolutely ensures you'll meet your savings goals. Paying yourself first makes YOU and your long term financial health the top priority! The highly disciplined person can divide his or her earnings into emergency funds and investments. Others who are not as highly disciplined can set up automatic deposits from payroll or even automatic drafts from your checking account into an investment every month. Buying a home using your VA benefit could be considered an easy application of this concept because your mortgage is paying down principal loan balance every month. Paying yourself first is challenging, we know, but the discipline equals success, stability and wealth.

As investment professionals, we often hear counter-arguments to the concept of paying yourself first such as, "Yeah, right!" Reluctant savers spew resistance as strong as bitter coffee, "Which do I sacrifice in order to save? My baby's food? Or shelter?" We understand such worry, but stand by the savings mantra. You

CAN save, even if you have to "find" money to save. Here are a few ideas to get you started.

- Set up an automatic deposit to take a percentage of your income off the top of your paycheck and place it directly into an investment account. A 401K or Thrift Savings Plan account are common examples.
- Budget. Create a budget and stick to it. Are there purchases like unread magazine subscriptions, premium cable channels and online subscriptions that might not be as important as you once though they were?
- When you get your next raise, save the amount of that raise and continue to live off your previous income and budget. Save and invest the difference.
- Have more than one income stream (e.g., second job, a hobby that brings in some extra cash) and bank one of them.
- Eat at home rather than spend $25-$100 dining out. Instead, save that money. Tip: instead of ordering take out, cook a week's worth of meals on the weekend and freeze them. Each night, defrost a meal and enjoy better food that is less expensive.
- Quit Starbucks. There's nothing more aggravating than someone pointing out that a $5 latte every day is money down the drain, money you could gather and invest. Coffee brewed at home in a travel mug is a big step towards financial independence.
- Quit smoking. Again, do the math. There is every reason on Earth to quit. Money is just one of them.
- Save your change. While it might sound too simple, give this a shot. At the end of every day, put the coins in your pocket into a jar for a year. At the end of that year, roll the coins, deposit them in the bank and write a check to your

investment company. You will be amazed at the amount of
money you've inadvertently saved.

When you pay yourself first, that means that every month
you're contributing towards some sort of savings plan and/or
investment. Begin by planning for the unplanned.

Establish an Emergency Fund

Having an emergency fund is so important. Not to shock you,
but a health crisis or a single trip to the ER could wipe you out
financially and could drive you into bankruptcy. You need to start
and continue to grow an emergency fund for "rainy days." Other,
non-medical emergencies will come up and you'll need immediate
cash to fix the problem, and you won't be able to just draw from
funds you've earmarked for rent and other necessities.

How much should you plan to have in your emergency fund?
It depends on your situation. If you net 5K a month after your
payroll deductions, you really should have at least 15K in the bank
for emergencies. Say you get sick and can't work, or you lose
your job and can't find a new one. What then? What if your skills
are highly specialized and you need to cover a whole year's worth
of expenses because it will take that long to find just the right new
position? In this case, you should have 60K in the bank!

The less stable your career or the less consistent your income
is such as a commissioned income, the more you should save. On
the other hand, if you have a secure job, such as a government
position, or have longevity at a successful corporation, you might
only need the equivalent of three month's pay as an emergency
fund. Regardless of your scenario, create an emergency fund and
then start investing for retirement. Starting with the creation of the

emergency fund first is important. You don't want to start a tax-qualified investment and then raid it because of an emergency. Now that that the "unplanned" is planned for, let's talk about the end game – retirement planning.

It's very important to learn how to invest your savings. Investing is not only for the wealthy. It is for everyone who hopes and plans to be fiscally stable, even rich. You need to begin investing NOW, so you can make money and live off of your investments later, as opposed to still trying to work at the end of your productive years in life. If you start young, you now know the amount of wealth you can build over a lifetime.

Investment Categories and "Vehicles"

Based on your investment goals, you must make choices regarding investment categories such as stocks, bonds, mutual funds or real estate. You can then break down your decisions further into investment vehicles. In the stock market, you might consider a portfolio of individual stocks, where each stock is your "vehicle" to achieve your goal. Or a particular mutual fund concentrating on smaller, high growth companies could be your vehicle in the market. Or if you like real estate, perhaps your vehicle of choice is a real estate investment trust or REIT. These are professionally managed funds that invest in commercial real estate for you.

Some mutual funds have created heroic returns for their investors! One of the most popular mutual funds in history is called Fidelity Magellan. The world renowned money manager Peter Lynch managed this fund for twenty three years. During his tenure, Peter Lynch reportedly averaged an amazing 29.2% average annual return for his fund shareholders. Incredible! And now I have to add a plug for my dear 'ole dad. In the January 1997 issue of Forbes magazine, my father Van L. Brady of Presidio Management was compared to Peter Lynch. My dad was a great professional investor who performed exceptionally well for his limited partners of Presidio.

Tax Qualified Investing

As you are making your investment decisions, it is very advantageous to implement strategic tax planning by placing those "vehicles" into a tax qualified status or "tax advantaged" status such as a 401k or IRA. The tax qualified plan is like the garage that you park your investment vehicle into. For almost all of your investment choices, you could open an IRA (Individual Retirement Account) with a custodian or directly with a company such as Fidelity Investments as your custodian. You should nearly always choose a tax qualified account to start with until those account options are exhausted. Because of IRS limits on the total amount you are allowed to contribute, you might have more money to invest than the account limits allow, and THAT's the position you want to be in!

Now let's discuss some convenient investment plans you can look into right now. The first one, that you want to take maximum advantage of, is your company retirement plan, especially if they match your contributions. A 401(k) plan might be offered by your company and administered by a party outside the company, and the funds are managed by a fund company such as Fidelity.

Employer Matching Programs

Employer matching programs exist to provide incentives to the employee, as a bonus for a job well done. They build employee loyalty, and allow the company to get certain tax breaks.

If your company says, "You put in 6% of your gross income, and we'll match you dollar per dollar and also put in 6% of your gross income into your 401(k)." That's HUGE! You have to take advantage of that. There are some 401(k) programs where employees can put in as much as 15% of their gross income and their company will match 7%. THAT'S phenomenal! It's FREE MONEY! So if you can max out your 401(k) contributions and have your company match it, do it! Maximize that retirement contribution!

Simple Investment Categories

When you've earmarked funds to invest in retirement planning and wealth building, you'll need to educate yourself on various investment category options and decide where to place your hard earned money. To make it simple, mutual fund investments of stocks and bonds could be categorized into three types of funds:

- Growth – typically all stocks.
- Income – typically all bonds.
- Balanced (Growth and Income Fund).

Growth typically means more "growth oriented stocks" that are focused on re-investing the earnings and not paying dividends to shareholders. Higher returns are expected by shareholders because they are willing to accept more price volatility and risk.

Income typically means a basket of corporate bonds, municipal bonds and or mortgages that generate income to pay out to their shareholders. Lower returns are expected by shareholders and they are willing to accept less price volatility and less risk.

Balanced (Growth and Income) are typically a combination of growth stocks, divided-paying stocks, and a mix of corporate bonds and mortgages. Investors interested in this category are typically in transition from their productive earning years to their retirement years. They are transitioning from assuming more risk to accepting lower potential returns and less risk.

As you approach retirement, hopefully your income will come less from salary and more from some type of income generating instrument, such as bonds. As you approach age fifty five and have ten to fifteen years left in the workforce (based on the traditional idea of retiring at age sixty five), any financial planner will suggest that your portfolio mix be more balanced, such as a mix of dividend paying stocks and bonds.

If there isn't a 401(k) program you can participate in through your company, then you need to start looking at other tax qualified programs on your own. Individual Retirement Accounts are the most popular choice. There are two types - **Traditional IRA** and **Roth IRA**.

Traditional IRA

A traditional Individual Retirement Account, or IRA, is a tax deductible AND a tax deferred investment account. You are allowed to contribute "pre-tax" dollars into the account (certain income limitations may apply) which means that your contributions are deducted from your gross taxable income. This saves on the tax bite, and then the contributions grow tax deferred. You pay income taxes when the funds are withdrawn in your retirement years. Tax deferred growth is a HUGE advantage when compounding returns over a lifetime. If the taxing authorities were extracting funds to pay taxes along the way, your account value would not grow at nearly the rate it will when taxes are deferred.

Also, there are mandatory withdrawal schedules once you hit a particular age, currently age seventy and a half. The IRS MAKES you withdraw the funds so they can receive the tax revenue.

Roth IRA

Financial advisors have differing opinions on Traditional IRA vs. Roth IRA. Your current tax bracket and your anticipated retirement tax bracket should play a role in your decision to chose one status vs another. Speculating on your tax bracket at retirement is just that…speculation. But as an investor, you must make a guess. The main difference between the Roth IRA and the traditional IRA (and other retirement plans that are "tax advantaged") is that with the Roth, the contribution is not tax deductible, but no income taxes are assessed when the money is withdrawn!

There are many other "tax advantaged" accounts available to the interested investor. Some include: SEP-IRA, Simple-IRA; Solo 401k and a Keogh plan. Most of these plans are geared toward retirement planning for the self-employed. Nearly all investment vehicles can be placed under or into an IRA or Roth IRA, especially using custodians that specialize in "self-directed" plans. It is not uncommon to invest in real estate, gold or other alternative investments with the help of these custodians.

Tax-free Growth Inside an Insurance Policy

I'm not a big fan of bundling investment products with insurance products in the same strategy, but sometimes a case CAN be made to do so. Traditional bundled insurance products began with "whole life insurance" more than a century ago.

Prudential and New York Life built massive businesses with these products as their foundations. In the seventies and eighties, as interest rates skyrocketed, these companies created new products such as "variable life" and "universal life" insurance. I'm still not a big fan. "Buy term (life insurance) and invest the difference" is a common mantra for folks who would prefer to separate insurance needs from investment needs. History has proven that investment yields inside insurance policies differ from that of traditional investment products not offered by insurance companies. Additionally, life insurance premiums are far less expensive when buying term insurance.

However, if you have exhausted all your tax-qualified possibilities and opportunities, the only other potential vehicle to grow income tax-free is inside an insurance policy. Insurance agents offer what they call "investment grade" insurance policies where an investor can grow their money tax-free. When the face value (of the life insurance benefit) is low and contributions are high, little is applied to the payment of the insurance premium and most of the investor's cash is applied to the investment inside the policy. This "investment grade" structure produces a product focusing on the merits of the investment and much less on the insurance benefit.

There exists limits on the minimization of the life insurance benefit vs. cash contributions to maintain the definition of "insurance," and thus, the beneficial tax treatment. With traditional whole life insurance, or cash value insurance, there's a life insurance component and a cash accumulation component bundled together. Whole life insurance is structured to focus on the insurance benefit. But within an investment grade insurance policy, the opposite is true. You're minimizing the insurance component and maximizing the cash component to focus on the anticipated investment results. Use these tax-free policies to your advantage if you have exhausted all other tax-free growth and investment options.

Investing in insurance products like life insurance and annuities inside the tax qualified status of an IRA, Roth IRA or other tax qualified plan is a waste of resources. Insurance products already have "tax advantaged" status. Keep these insurance products away from your retirement plans!

For assistance in fundamental financial planning, contact a financial planning professional, or let SoCalVAHomes help. Call us at 888-556-2018.

Chapter 27: Be a Real Estate Investor Using your VA Home Loan Benefit

How to use your VA Home Loan Benefit to immediately become a real estate investor

Yes! You can become a real estate investor using your VA Home Loan Benefit. In some circumstances, this can be accomplished where you can effectively end up living rent free! Let me explain. First, you will need to find a two, three, or four unit property (known as a "4-plex" consisting of four units in one building.) When your VA offer is accepted, simply choose your favorite unit to live in and rent out the other three units. If the economics work out correctly, you can use your tenants' rent to pay your mortgage, property tax, insurance and other expenses. If their rents cover all of that, then you can live rent free, with some other significant advantages and benefits as well.

Let's plug some numbers into this concept and see how the ideal transaction might look on paper:

You purchase a 4-Unit property for $500,000 and decide to live in Unit A.

Your monthly payment on a $500,000 loan with taxes and insurance is $3,000.

You rent Units B, C, and D for $1000 apiece.

In a perfect world, you won't have any vacancies and you'll get $3000 a month in tenant rent, which just happens to be your mortgage payment.

Therefore, you now live rent free in Unit A.

Even if the numbers aren't perfect, and you have to pay part of the mortgage on your 4-plex out of your own pocket, our recommendation is to seriously consider it. This piece of property can be part of a growing investment portfolio. And as rents typically go up over time, the rental income on just the three units could eventually cover your entire mortgage payment at some point in time. And if you ever decide to live somewhere else, the cash flow could be very attractive! And if the property appreciates…well that's a home run!!! That's investing!

From the example above, it would be an intelligent decision to pay as much as $1000/month out of your own pocket to cover your mortgage, your taxes, and your insurance. That would equal the rent you would pay anyway. Your tenants are covering the remaining expenses, and you still get the tax benefits and potential appreciation benefits! This is your money and your VA benefit working for you, and you've probably got the best unit in the property, perhaps even rent free.

Qualifying and Building Wealth

To qualify for a $3000/month mortgage payment, typically you are going to have to earn $8000-$10,000 a month. But here is the best part! Because the three rental units generate rental income, current VA underwriting guidelines allow you use 75% of that rental income to off-set the mortgage payments, even without any previous real estate investment experience. This is a big deal because conventional underwriting guidelines don't allow you to do that unless you already have real estate investment experience demonstrated by a Schedule E on your tax returns. In general, even though your income might not be large, you could buy a more expensive property because you are using the rental income from the units you're not living in to qualify for the mortgage. This allows you to build wealth using your VA Home Loan Benefit!

Again, with a small income that is used to qualify, you can control a relatively large asset, benefitting from the property's appreciation. It is really a great wealth building tool, where you might only qualify for a $200,000 single family home but you can also qualify for a $500,000 four-plex. Both are going to appreciate in a similar manner. If property appreciates by 10% you are going to be up $50K on the

4-plex but only $20K on your house. That's "leverage!" Leverage is the concept of controlling a large asset with borrowed money. In this example, your asset is "100% leveraged." You've acquired and controlled it with entirely borrowed money. This is how the wealthy made their money before software, the internet and social media start-ups...they bought stocks and real estate!

For assistance in becoming a real estate investor using your VA loan, let SoCalVAHomes help. Call us at 888-556-2018.

Chapter 28: A Veteran's Vision...How To Start a Business

Using your VA Benefits to start a business – chasing the American Dream.

One way to avoid unemployment is...to start your own business! The essence of developing an idea and starting a business can be described in simple terms. Entrepreneurs find a need and create solutions. They create a product or service to fulfill that need. Entrepreneurs also see the deficiencies and draw backs in some products. They see products that have room for improvement, and they create better versions of that product or service! Some ideas change whole industries and change the way we live. Technology advances are classic examples. Once we played our music from vinyl, then next it was tape...and then came digital and low cost music sharing! But it doesn't have to be technology that is the change. Uber and Lyft are ride-sharing "game changers," on their way to eliminating an entire industry of transportation – taxis and shuttles.

Another way to start a business is just to model someone else. Repeating a success story has been done countless time before. Actually, you don't need to be original to be successful! Find some help! There are literally thousands of mentors willing to help you along your path – for FREE. You can find them at places such as SCORE, an organization consisting of retired business people who volunteer their time to be mentors. We will talk more about SCORE in this chapter.

It may be hard to understand at first, but pursing your dreams is about the journey, not necessary the destination. Initial struggles will evolve into long term strength. Look at every "no" and failure along the way as an opportunity to change course and find a "yes," discovering success. Don't listen to friends, family and negative influences who tell you it can't be done. Becoming a student of marketing is invaluable. You'll need to attract and retain customers and clients to your business. Keep asking yourself tough questions, be persistent…and most of all…enjoy the ride!

Did you know that you can call the VA for resources on starting you own business? A toll-free call center is available at 1-866-584-2344, where Veterans, military personnel or their family members can talk one-on-one with a business coach about how to start or expand a business. Topics and information include:

- Information on business management, financing and marketing, as well as small-business conferences and business training opportunities.

- Information about legislation affecting Veteran-owned business, including existing laws that require federal agencies to increase business opportunities for Veterans by setting aside a certain portion of their purchasing dollars for Veterans and service-disabled Veterans.

- Inclusion in a Veteran's business database for exposure to commercial and government business, plus recognition as a verified Veteran-owned or service-disabled Veteran-owned small business.

Who Qualifies to Access these Resources:

- Veterans.

- Service-disabled Veterans.
- Active-duty service members who are eligible for the military's Transition Assistance Program.
- Reservists and National Guard members.
- Current spouses of any of the above.
- The widowed spouse of a service member or Veteran who died during service or of a service-connected disability.

In general, starting your business can be broken down into simple steps and the VA has programs to assist you with each step.

1. Prepare a written outline of your idea.

2. Establish your business structure. A business must be formed within some kind of legal framework or as a sole proprietor. Determining the correct entity in which to form your business may be a challenging process. Your entity structure will affect the way you file your taxes. Your business will be officially "organized" within a specific state. A Small Business Development Center can assist you with state registration forms. To learn more about legal structure and business tax concerns go to IRS.gov. The alternative to all this is simply a "Sole Proprietorship." You would report your revenue, expenses and net earnings or losses on Schedule "C" of your federal tax returns. If you organize a business entity, it will require its own tax ID.

3. Prepare a business plan. This is a complex process that will become the blueprint of how you will run your business, market your business, and determine the funding requirements and viability of your new

business.

4. Have a business counselor review your business plan.
    The Association of Small Business Development
    Centers offers free consulting and low cost training to
    help new entrepreneurs realize their dream of business
    ownership, and to assist existing businesses on how to
    remain competitive in the complex marketplace of an
    ever-changing global economy. To find the nearest
    SBDC to you, go to: http://www.asbdc-us.org/ ;
    http://americassbdc.org/ or visit score.org and get
    connected with a free, successful, tech savvy mentor!

5. Implement the business plan. The Small Business
    Administration's (SBA) website has information on
    starting a business at www.sba.gov and SCORE
    score.org is part of the SBA. SCORE is a valuable
    volunteer organization of retired business men and
    women available to mentor and guide you.

6. Register your Veteran-owned small business on the
    Vendor Information Pages (VIP) database
    (www.vetbiz.gov) of Veteran entrepreneurs.

7. The Department of Veterans Affairs has created the
    Center for Veterans Enterprise (CVE), which is solely
    dedicated to assisting Veterans in starting and building
    businesses. They maintain a web site that serves as the
    federal government portal for veteran-owned businesses
    known as vetbiz.gov.

Government Contracting

Did you know the U.S. Federal Government buys nearly $100 billion worth of goods and services from small businesses each year? Government contracts can offer significant opportunities for small businesses, but selling to the government requires a very different approach than selling to the commercial sector.

The SBA has created a series of free online contracting courses designed to help prospective and existing small businesses understand the basics about contracting with governmental agencies. Whether you're just getting started or looking for ways to compete more successfully in the government contracting marketplace, check out the courses.

Government agency procurement officers have certain socioeconomic goals to meet in terms of the number of Veteran-owned, woman-owned, disadvantaged, and small businesses they work with. For example, if you're a Veteran-owned, woman-owned, disadvantaged small business you offer three socioeconomic "points" to any agency that hires you. You should certainly discuss your VOB (Veteran Owned Business) status in conversations and through relationships.

Some additional resources include SCORE's Veterans Fast Start Program which offers:

- **FREE Simple Steps Workshop:** Get FREE access to the Simple Steps for Starting Your Business Workshop Series (or equivalent). It is five-part series will take you through the basics of entrepreneurship and pair you with a mentor to help you test the feasibility of your business idea.

- **FREE Business Mentoring:** SCORE has over 13,000 mentors across 500 industries and is prime source for free and confidential business advice for small business entrepreneurs - in person at one of their chapters or online.

- **FREE Online Workshops:** Theseare available 24 hours a day, 7 days a week on a variety of business topics to aid with your business planning.

- FREE Templates & Tools: SCORE offers hundreds of free business templates, calculators, spreadsheets, document templates, tips and other resources to help you in your planning and operations.

Your Entity Set-Up is Important

Once you have your idea written down and its feasibility tested, you may want to sit down with a CPA and go over what kind of business structure and entity you need for both liability and tax advantages. Common choices are:

- **S-Corp:** Primarily taxed as a "pass through" to you as personal income.
- **C-Corp:** Next level "up." Corporate taxes with more protection from creditors and business liabilities.
- **LLC:** Limited Liability Company – very common structure, easy organization.
- **LP:** Limited Partnership – less common; limited personal liability

Again, a "Sole Proprietorship" may work for you requiring

none of these set-up options. You'll certainly want to give some consideration to what state you'll file your entity in. That research will focus on where you are located, what product or service you are offering, where you are selling or offering it, and where your clients or customers reside. It will also include consideration of state entity taxation and entity maintenance fees with that state.

All entities are relatively easy to set up directly with the Secretary of State in each State in the union. Many filings can be completed online within minutes. Often, businesses file in Delaware. However, your business structure and IRS guidelines may disallow this.

You don't *need* a company like Legal Zoom or an attorney to file the paperwork for you. It's actually very simple. Once you find the business section for the secretary of state in the state you want to file (google "SOS + state"), find the forms to complete and start your desired entity structure. Search the current entities to make sure your business name is not already selected. With our real estate investment company, SARTRE, we filed more than twenty entities in five different states. The process was very easy and became routine very quickly.

Once you have your entity registered with the state (although you could probably reverse the steps, if you knew the name was available), go to IRS.gov, search and apply for a tax ID number (TIN) within the site. The IRS will instantly issue your entity a tax ID number online. You will need a tax ID Number to set up bank accounts in that business name. Again, you don't need an attorney. But you can get additional advice!

Additional Resources

- Financial Advice from CPAs. AICPA is connecting Veterans with CPAs across the country to provide up to FIVE hours of FREE financial advice to Veterans on starting or growing their business. Review the AICPA's CPA Volunteer Directory to find a CPA who best meets your needs.

- DOCSTOC - free trial of thousands of templates. DOCSTOC is a community for people to find and share professional documents used to start, grow, and manage their professional life and small business.

- Microsoft Special Offer. How could this resource list be complete without something from the largest software giant? Learn about a no-cost voucher for technology skills training and certification at **https://www.microsoft.com/learning/en-us/offers.aspx.**

- Rocket Lawyer: FIVE FREE LEGAL DOCUMENTS. Rocket Lawyer™ makes legal services easy and accessible for everyone, allowing you to customize legal documents that can be downloaded and shared instantly.

- FREE Veterans Group Edition licenses: Veterans Group Edition licenses, good for up to three users, for one year, free of charge.

- FREE Credit Card Reader: Square.com seems to work pretty well. Process credit card charges by attaching card reader to a smart phone or iPad.

- Finding funding for your business: Grants.gov offers free money allocated to help special groups of people.

- SBA Patriot Express is a new loan program for the Veteran community. The U.S. Small Business Administration has announced the SBA's Patriot Express Pilot Loan Initiative for Veterans and members of the military community wanting to establish or expand small businesses. Eligible military community members include: Veterans, Service-disabled Veterans, Active-duty service members eligible for the military's Transition Assistance Program, Reservists and National Guard members, current spouses of any of the above, and the widowed spouse of a service member or Veteran who died during service or of a service-connected disability. The SBA and its resource partners are focusing additional efforts on counseling and training to augment this loan initiative. Patriot Express loan proceeds can be used for most business purposes including:
  - Start up costs
  - Equipment purchases
  - Business-occupied real-estate purchases
  - Inventory
  - Infusing working capital
  - Managing your business
  - Expansion
  - Preparing your business for the possibility of your deployment
  - Setting up to sell goods and services to the government
  - Recovery from declared disasters.

Patriot Express loans feature the SBA's lowest interest rates for business loans, generally depending upon the size and maturity of the loan, with terms as long as thirty years. Your local SBA district office will have a listing of Patriot Express lenders in your area.

Epilogue: Can You Help Us?

Faced with an infinite uphill battle, SoCalVAHomes maintains an intense commitment to expand and find creative ways to serve those who served us.

The business model of choosing to exclusively serve active military and Veterans is a very dangerous decision. We have made an active choice that, from the viewpoint of an outsider, may look like business suicide! But we discovered a cause…more than a worthy mission…we want to "right a wrong."

The MOST DESERVING homebuyers in the marketplace are **those who serve…YOU.** YOU WERE THE MOST UNDERSERVED, the most snubbed, the most rejected by the real estate marketplace when using your VA home loan benefit, attempting to accomplish your goals and achieve your dreams. And it isn't your fault! *It is simple economics, market supply and demand in action…**and it was tragic in my view.***

With all of our programs, our goal is to eliminate the disadvantages Veterans face when buying homes. To gain a competitive advantage for our clients over and above the "average VA deal," we created our proprietary suite of programs which marry your VA loan with serious extra horsepower, so you can get the home you want, the home you deserve. When we entered into this market with new and innovative ideas, we were purely motivated to simply correct "the wrong," dissolve this disadvantage, and turn the tables.

Defying "smart" business decisions, we choose to work with you, a collective group primarily made up of first time homebuyers who typically buy entry level homes in the lower price ranges of Southern California neighborhoods and therefore generate the lowest relative income per transaction. Pure economics would suggest that this provides our company with the least opportunity for economic success, stacking the odds against us. We choose to serve you, in general a clientele that typically has a lower range of credit qualifications making it more challenging for our clients to qualify to buy a home. We choose to embrace you, a group that the housing market perceives as the riskiest buyers, most likely to take the longest to close or ultimately fall out of escrow and cancel! When utilizing our Veteran's Angel Program, our job is to convince the listing agent and seller otherwise!

Motivated home buyers using their VA home loan benefit to purchase are a tiny percentage of the overall buyers in the market.

That makes YOU pretty hard to find! Finding you is a lot like looking for a needle in a haystack! I know this through lots of trial and error! In the last five years, I've tried every possible means you might imagine to reach out to you. From our original SoCalVAhomes van (used for our client's Dreamweaver projects) to bus ads, to church bulletins, direct mail targeted to Camp Pendleton, to realtors (who didn't want to work with Veterans), to real estate magazines, to KFI radio ads (Oooh, that was expensive!), to Facebook, Google, Twitter, to actually soliciting doctors' offices who took TRICARE (so they could pass out flyers). Yes, we've tried it all, and you are hard to find!

And to do all the things that we do on our Dreamweaver Home Purchase Process™ is very, very difficult. Frankly, I find all this…ALL OF IT…to be the most extraordinary and exciting challenge – the largest I've ever faced in my life. I pray every day that I have the strength, stamina and endurance, the courage and creativity to see it through – to do the greatest good for the maximum number of Veterans and active military families. We can't help everyone, but we are very committed to help you.

To accomplish our goals, to help large numbers of Veterans and active military families in local Southern California communities purchase the right homes, we will need lots of help. To expand, we will need lots of licensed field agents. Our Property Acquisition Specialists, on the ground looking at homes, are the hardest working people and the most integral players to achieving success for our clients. Please help us by referring potential candidates for field agents!

Again, finding qualified, motivated buyers wanting to use their VA loan to buy a home is not easy. It's very difficult. We need your help! Please refer your friends, family, superiors, subordinates and other Veterans to us, so we can help them achieve their home buying goals! Ask us about any promotions and referral programs we may currently have!

We see our relationship with our clients as a partnership. We don't view ourselves and our company simply as service providers. We are much, MUCH more than that! With all of our proprietary programs, we take far more business risk and direct, financial risk for you than anyone or any other company that we are aware of. And we need your help and support. Please get the word out, and please go to our website to subscribe to my AH!HA! INFO – ENTERTAINMENT letter. This is a six-times a year company communication. It's additional education, and it's very entertaining! Thank you so much for your belief and support.

Respectfully,

About The Author

After attaining his bachelor's degree in business economics from University of California at Santa Barbara, Peter Van L. Brady began his financial services career in 1987 and previously held an insurance license and Series 3, 6, & 63 securities licenses.

Attaining his real estate license in 1992, Mr. Brady began a career in residential lending. Financing consultations with his clients throughout Southern California always came from the perspective of meeting financial planning goals. His lending career milestones included: Co-founding One Touch Lending in 1996, creating and servicing a significant portfolio of "private" second mortgages and providing personal career coaching to mortgage brokers who wanted to duplicate his success.

In 2008, Mr. Brady co-founded SARTRE LLC, a real estate investment company which, in its first three years of operation, bought and sold over 1000 homes throughout the U.S. SARTRE then participated in purchasing, renovating and exiting investments in more than 1700 multi-family apartment and condo units in Southern Florida.

After making VA loans to active military and Veterans since 9/11, in the summer of 2011, Peter founded SoCalVAHomes.org to create a home buying advantage for Veterans. He developed the Dreamweaver Home Purchase Process™, which allowed home buyers to purchase fully, custom renovated homes for zero down and zero closing costs using their VA home loan benefit. He then developed his company's Veterans Angel Program and brought to market the "build your own home," VA construction financing program.

He lives in San Clemente with his wife Nancy, where he enjoys jogging on the beach trail and surfing. He also found a passion for the extra large waves at Todos Santos, Mexico. Nancy and Peter have two daughters Chelsea and Mia. They also have Nicholas, an adult son with autism, who currently remains at home.

Made in the USA
San Bernardino, CA
26 January 2017